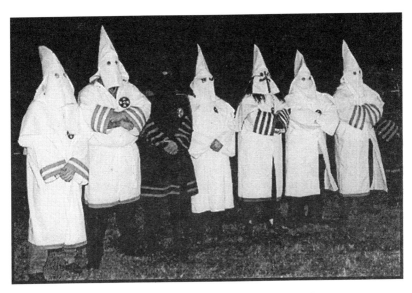

T *hat historians should give their own country a break, I grant you; but not so as to state things contrary to fact. For there are plenty of mistakes made by writers out of ignorance, and which any man finds difficult to avoid. But, if we knowingly write what is false, whether for the sake of our country or our friends or just to be pleasant, what difference is there between us and hack writers? Readers should be very attentive to and critical of historians, and they in turn should be constantly on their guard.*
—Polybius, 208-126 BC

Acknowledgments:

I deeply thank my wife, children and parents for being my cheerleaders and proofreaders; Deborah Cafiero for urging me to write and rewrite until I found my voice; Patsy Sims for being gracious and encouraging; Frances Beresford for teaching me how to do this; Rick Beresford for his pizza; Jay Van Dyke who patiently and professionally walked me through the many technical steps to get this book to the printer; and Brad Thompson who gave me his trust and friendship.

I would be remiss not to thank the many Klansmen and women who gave freely of their time, who treated me with respect and without suspicion, asking nothing more than that I do my best to tell the truth.

Worth Weller
October, 1998

List of Illustrations
and Photo Credits

Brad Thompson (center) responding to hecklers by taking off his hood *(photo courtesy Bryan, Ohio, Times)* .... Cover

Back cover photographs by Worth H. Weller

Table of Contents

Introduction:
Flirting with the Devil

Deeply troubled by the course upon which I was embarking—the co-authorship of a book explaining in personal detail the inner workings of the modern Ku Klux Klan—I took solace one Saturday evening in the thoughts of others who have by choice or chance crossed into unfamiliar territory where the only guide is one's own moral compass.

To be truthful, I was a little frightened, not by the thought of the guns and rough rhetoric of these angry people who dare to don hoods and

Klan Rally, LaGrange, Indiana, 1996

burn crosses in the 1990's, but rather by the anticipation of brushing so closely with people who journalists and historians clearly consider beyond the pale.

Would I become contaminated?

Would I write a contaminated book?

The first question my wife asked me upon learning I intended to travel the following weekend in the company of the Imperial Wizard of the American Knights of the Ku Klux Klan to a rally he promised would bring out an angry mob of Chicago-area blacks and Hispanics, was "How do you feel about that?"

I told her honestly, "Not very good."

Not overly concerned about my own safety—my earlier experience with Klan rallies had made me realize it was generally safer to be on the Klan side of the police line than anywhere else—I was instead gravely concerned about my own integrity, as well as my ability to tell a truthful, unbiased story. Would I paint these people as the idiots most presume they are, even if I learned otherwise? Or worse, given my tendency to believe in the general good nature of all human beings, would I find myself liking them and overlooking their hateful behavior?

Being a congenital optimist, I generally forgive quirkiness and find myself even drawn to it. In my thirty years as a journalist I have interviewed two murderers. One cold-bloodedly blew his wife's chest off with a shotgun after he dragged her out of the bed of an Indiana barkeeper, and the other to this day denies her deed, despite the evidence that convinced a Colorado jury otherwise. I like both these people, would gladly be seen in a restaurant eating dinner with them, and found myself laughing and feeling empathetic during the hours I spent with them in jail.

Similarly and more recently, during the winter of 1996, I spent some time in southern Mexico as a human rights observer, living in a remote Mayan village high in the cloud forests of Chiapas. My job was to accompany the indigenous villagers and to document any illegal actions of the nearby Mexican army, which maintained a heavily fortified outpost supplied only by helicopter, as no passable roads traversed those jungles. One day I trudged through the torpid heat to the top of a hill, where a sandbagged bunker maintained its ominous vigilance over our motley collection of thatched and tin-roofed huts. I was simply curious. I wanted to see for myself what these soldiers were like, to know just a little better these heavily armed, grim-faced men who had been accused of the worst of atrocities towards the traditional Mayan people. Looking beyond their camouflage fatigues and flak jackets, ignoring their German-made Hockler assault rifles, I discovered young men—almost boys—as grateful for a smile and a friendly word as any other human being.

So what would I find when I hung out with the Klan?

Knowing that soon enough I would discover my own answers as I traveled with these robed men and women to their rallies and cross burnings, I deliberately turned away from the great historical analyses of the Klan, mostly written as academic tomes or documentary treatises compiled from news accounts of the period, and instead sought answers among my favorite authors and historical figures.

Will and Ariel Durant, in their *Lessons of History*, written in 1968, assured me I would find people who had contributed to civilization just as had those who came before them. They warned me I should treat them with respect, for they would be contributing in their own way.

Mexican soldiers chasing Zapatista guerillas in the rain (Chiapas, 1996)

"A knowledge of history may teach us that civilization is a cooperative product, that nearly all peoples have contributed to it," they write in their chapter on Race and History. "The civilized soul will reveal itself in treating every man or woman, however lowly, as a representative of one of these creative and contributor groups."

Were the Durants warning me not to look down my nose at these people? It's doubtful, of course, that the Durants were thinking of the Klan when they wrote these words, but I was struck by their implication. The modern Klan is as much, if not more so, a part of our unfolding history as any other minority group. So who would be the judge of their impact on our civilization? This book in no way attempts to paint the Klan as having a positive message,

Edna Berry

but the impact Klan rallies have had on their targeted communities is explored.

Equally as troubling to me as my own fear of intellectual contamination, was my failure to understand what was drawing me to these people with their outlandish costumes, hateful tattoos and strident voices.

Sure, I was smug in my knowledge that I embraced diversity. My best friend in college thirty years ago was a homosexual. One of my closest friends in this small, lily white, 99.8 percent Christian town I have called my own for over two decades is Jewish. But what really did I know? Didn't I enjoy red neck jokes just a little too much? Wasn't my "hatred" of all things right-wing more than a tad hypocritical? A little voice kept warning me not to be quite so sure I wasn't blind to my own prejudices.

Arthur Schlesinger, Jr., writing in his 1986 *Cycles of American History*, had his own warnings for me.

Speaking of the lack of forthrightness in our own national political dialog, in which indiscriminate bombing runs over Hanoi (substitute today Baghdad) are called "surgical strikes" and the gun toting thugs who killed innocent villagers in Nicaragua during the Contra War were called "freedom fighters", he notes: "Vietnam and then Watergate left a good many Americans with a hatred of doubletalk and a hunger for bluntness and candor."

The Klan, as these pages will reveal, is nothing if not blunt and candid. With eerie prescience to our own political age of Clintonesque double speak about sex and lies, Schlesinger adds, "In this season of semantic malnutrition, who is not grateful for a public voice that blurts out what the speaker honestly believes?"

My own fear, far beyond any dim feelings of bodily threat at either the hands of protestors who might mistake me for a Klan sympathizer or from a Klansman who might accurately sense my disdain, was that I would show grudging respect, both in my writing and in my interviewing. I might inadvertently honor these people who did away with indecipherable doublespeak to shout out their honestly held beliefs, most often in the face of hostile crowds. (Of course, as these pages also reveal, it is a little easier to take an unpopular stand when you are assured of protection by phalanxes of state police and county sheriff's deputies and when you are cordoned off from those who disagree with you by barriers of blazing orange construction fence.)

Speaking of semantic malnutrition, the Klan's language is indeed not malnourished. It is with reluctance, and apology, that I use their own language in some of these pages. I have tried to restrict such use to just a chapter or two, for their language often goes well beyond colorful. It is not only offensive in many cases, it is downright grating and degrading, both to hear and to read. For repeating it in Chapter Two, I apologize. It was with considerable anguish that I listened to tapes over and over again to get the language accurate, and it is with some degree of shame that I repeat it here. However, my intent in this book, as I told the Klan upfront, was to let them tell their own story in their own words, with as little of my own editorializing as possible.

To honestly know about the modern Klan you have to hear their own voices, rough language and all.

So why go into it in the first place? Given the raw and abusive nature of the topic, some, including myself, would ask, "Is this book necessary?"

That's a good question. I'm not entirely convinced I can answer it to everyone's satisfaction, but what follows is my best effort.

Listening to their message—viewing tapes of their rallies and participating in two myself as a photographer and journalist—I was

Klan supportors, LaGrange, Indiana

constantly reminded of Lewis Carroll's *Alice Through the Looking Glass*. In this childhood classic, Alice puzzles over language in a book that looks oddly familiar but that she can't quite read. When she finally holds a looking glass up to the pages, she can read the sonorous poem, "Jabberwocky," only to realize to her dismay that although it is a great poem, the words fail to make sense. Humpty Dumpty, however, soon comes to her rescue. "When I use a word," Humpty Dumpty said in a rather scornful tone, "it means just what I choose it to mean—neither more nor less." Alice, somewhat in a huff, retorts, "The question is, whether you can make words mean so many different things."

Therein lies the allure of the Klan.

Shouting rhetoric from courthouse steps that stirs dim memories of our own shared history, modern Klansmen (and their women) skillfully belie the misconception that they are simply ignorant white trash. Quoting the Bible and the Constitution, they use familiar words to suit their own meanings.

In fact, as these pages will reveal, a Klan rally is much like an American History lesson seen through Alice's looking glass.

But beyond the childish allure of Klan rallies and their nightmarish cross "lightings" that often follow, is their own grim reminder that sets the theme for their late 1990's procession across the Midwest and central eastern states: "You can ignore us if you want to, but we'll always be here."

Is this a statement of truth or a threat? If it is true, then why is it true?

Journalist Bill Moyers and philosopher Joseph Campbell, in their book *The Power of Myth* give us a few clues. Moyers asks Campbell for an interpretation of these lines by William Butler Yeats in his poem "The Second Coming": "Turning and turning in the widening gyre/The falcon cannot hear the falconer;/Things fall apart; the centre cannot hold;/Mere anarchy is loosed upon the world,/The blood-dimmed tide is loosed..."

Campbell responds: "When you come to the end of one time and the beginning of a new one, it's a period of tremendous pain and turmoil."

Pain and turmoil. This indeed is the breeding ground always of the Ku Klux Klan. When one looks at the historical Klan—which is not the task of this book as that has been an exercise accomplished in an excellent variety of ways before (see bibliography)—a pattern emerges. Klan activities surface at times of change and disruption: the end of the Civil War, the beginning of new waves of immigration just after the turn of the century, the onset of the Depression, the 60's civil-rights era, and now the onslaught of the new global economy.

Leonard J. Moore in his 1991 historical analysis of the Ku Klux Klan in Indiana, *Citizen Klansmen,* found that Klan membership there soared wherever rural life and work styles were being threatened by urbanization, as was occurring in central and northern Indiana as the century changed. "The Klan was strongest in areas of Indiana that had been most altered by the process of industrial development," his statistical analysis revealed.

Thus the Klan historically is an opportunistic organization, growing and contracting in membership in response to the economic pulse of the times.

So, if their statement harshly screamed from the courthouse steps that the Klan will always be with us is a threat, do we have to be captive to that threat?

It is my hope that these pages will shed some light in the search to find some answers to that question.

Samuel Taylor Coleridge, writing in 1831, had similar hopes, although he wasn't very optimistic: "If men could learn from history, what lessons it might teach us! But passion and party blind our eyes, and the light which experience gives is a lantern on the stern, which shines only on the waves behind us!"

As I have indicated earlier, it is with a sense of apology that I offer up these pages. To anyone who feels I have acted as an apologist for the Klan, I plead for your forgiveness, as I have earnestly crafted every sentence, asked every question, with that fear in mind. And to those who feel I have unjustly vilified and stereotyped an already marginalized people, so too I say that was not my intent and offer my apologies. My intent was to capture these hooded and angry people in their vulnerability as real, live, flesh and blood people— not as dim, shadowy figures of times gone by nor as numbers and charts in a sociology textbook.

Most important of course, to those who have been victimized by the Klan, both covertly and overtly, I understand that apologies do not suffice. I can only hope this book in some small way can be part of a reconciliation process.

Read these pages to discover wherein the Klan professes to find salvation, but rest assured that I firmly believe the Klan is on a path of mutual destruction. Our own salvation as a nation can be based only on honest recognition, acknowledgment and acceptance of our differences. No amount of time spent at rallies, no amount of camaraderie with Klansmen and women has changed my fervent belief that diversity brings not just richness, but is actually the lifeblood of a great people and a great nation.

Worth Weller
North Manchester, Indiana
September, 1998

Chapter One:
Rage Against the Machine

**The American Knights of the Ku Klux Klan,
LaGrange, Indiana, 1996**

When Brad Thompson's two-year old son Bart choked to death early one evening just before Thanksgiving of 1994, it never occurred to him that the Ku Klux Klan would rescue him from his sea of pain.

It never occurred to him that the Klan would be the natural outlet for the rage that had already been building up in him like the tides of the Red Sea which the hand of God separated for a lost people an eon ago.

Rage born of being lost in a sea of resentment.

Resentment born of frustration.

Frustration with his crummy mobile home with the heat vents

poking up through the blistered plywood floor.

Frustration with a child-bride barely half his age who wouldn't (or couldn't) care for his children from his first marriage let alone their own two toddlers.

Frustration with a dirty and dangerous foundry job that was all he could get despite his technical engineering degree. Frustration that he has to be grateful for this job staring at a machine all night. Grateful—and obliged—because the father of his teenaged bride got this job for him.

A job he has to cling to, accepting whatever hours come his way on whatever shift and weekend is available. Inconvenient hours he has to clock in for unfailingly if he hopes to get his head above water. If he hopes to move out of this crummy trailer park. If he hopes to drive anything but a rusted out Dodge minivan. If he hopes his sons won't have to take dirty, dangerous jobs at a foundry.

A job he goes to every night, head down, despite a home-life in turmoil with periodic welfare visits from nosy caseworkers who wonder how Bart got a broken leg that summer and who can't understand why Joey, just nine months younger, still isn't walking.

Despite a nagging fear that things just aren't quite right at home while he is away.

"Why is it I go to work leaving Bart happy and playing with his action figures in front of the TV only to come home in the morning and discover he has two black eyes? Leslie says he was playing with the door and fell down the steps. Hit the concrete pad face first, she says. But why didn't he land on his hands?" This is a tape that rewinds endlessly in Thompson's head as he sits night after night in front of his greasy, noisy molding machine.

Night after night, facing the boredom through the long, dark hours. All the while helplessly sensing his life is getting worse, not better.

Suspecting now—now that it's too late—that he was a fool to leave his wife Brenda of seventeen years. A fool to chase after a teenager not much older than his and Brenda's own two kids. A fool to leave one family behind and start a new family with two more children. Children who as much as he loves them are like a sea anchor that keeps him tied to his trashy mobile home and broken down cars and boring job, never getting ahead but only riding the waves of his tumultuous and dreary home life.

Children that he worries about constantly.

"What Leslie says is full of shit. Nothing's never Leslie's fault. But Bart still has two black eyes and Joey, Joey, I don't know. He just doesn't act right. Why don't he show no growth? He looks, he acts, like he lives in his crib all the time. When I'm at work don't no one play with him? And don't no one ever feed him?" Thompson's tape now is playing a mournful tune of guilt. And fear.

Fear of what he'll have to face when he drives home from work

American Knights filming protestors and the press at their LaGrange rally

the next morning and walks around the mud puddles to climb his steel steps and pushes back the battered screen door, hoping that when he peers into the gloomy and cluttered common cooking, eating and sitting area that marks mobile homes like his in thousands of cramped trailer parks all looking alike across the Midwest, he won't find Leslie waiting at the kitchen table, cigarette in hand dangling above a full, stinking ash tray, with more bad news.

Fear too, that anything he does to break the sick cycle of his second marriage—like staying home more from work to watch after the kids himself and to spend some time trying to talk reasonableness into Leslie—will jeopardize his well-paying but demanding job.

A job which is one of the few things in his life he can call a success story, displaying proudly to me three years later his most recent, framed certificate honoring him for twelve months of perfect job attendance.

For Thompson is no dummy. He knows his foundry job is a job he has to keep, no matter his persistent doubts about what goes on in his sagging double-wide when he isn't there to watch over his two dear sons.

In 1994 northeastern Indiana was only barely emerging from the social and economic chaos of the decade-long blight that blasted hopes and futures of working-class families throughout the rust belt of America's industrial heartland, leaving tens of thousands of workers like Brad Thompson disheartened and fearful. Well-paying jobs in Auburn or the other small towns that all look alike in the relentlessly rural landscape where Ohio, Michigan and Indiana join at the hip are like fine cigars. Hard to find and harder still to quit.

Thompson knew all too well that losing his foundry job meant minimum wage at McDonald's or Subway.

"This was a time of change and uncertainty in Indiana," reports Dr. Richard Harshbarger, economist at Manchester College, a small Midwestern liberal arts school just an hour's drive from Thompson's home. "NAFTA, globalization— these terms had very real meaning to the Hoosier workforce, as the better-paying jobs that didn't require much education all went fleeing south to Mexico, where wages weren't so high."

Harshbarger said that high school dropouts became overnight "virtually unemployable, with your basic C-average high school grad not faring much better."

He said this sudden economic shift in the workplace obviously implied social consequences. "People who were ripe for conspiracy theories, militias, that kind of thing, now they had evidence."

So Thompson's life was about to take an abrupt, but somewhat predictable, right turn.

Sociologists Betty Dobratz and Stephanie Shanks-Meile met scores of workers just like Brad Thompson in their research for their 1997 book, *White Power, White Pride*. In fact, they interviewed Thompson at a Klan rally he set up in Portage, Indiana, in May of 1996.

A common thread they found among members of the various elements of the white power groups in the United States is the sense of injustice they learned these people deeply feel. The sociologists uncovered a real fear of economic and social vulnerability among white separatists, who resent their perceived lack of power in the face of a threatening government and society. Not just an indifferent government and society, but one that is overtly hostile. One they feel is actively set against their economic and social status, illustrated in their minds by affirmative action programs, low-income housing, tolerance for gays, relaxed immigration laws, and the like.

"People in the white separatist movement argue that their deteriorating socioeconomic conditions are a consequence of racism against whites more than the result of general social processes that negatively affect most of us," they discovered after interviewing some 125 Ku Klux Klaners, Skinheads, Christian Identitists, and others in the white separatist movement. Those they interviewed didn't just fear loss of their white ethnic identity, they also feared "potential economic loss as they became less highly favored in an increasing number of social arenas." Marginal educations and lack of access to the political process cause these people to readily turn to "swift, simple solutions" with strong leadership from unconventional authority figures, the sociologists concluded.

In less academic words, 1994 was a very unsettling, practically helpless time for the likes of Brad Thompson, leaving him, even before the death of his son, very susceptible to the allure and promises of white separatist groups.

It was a time in which the one word that best described his world would be *frustration.*

Frustration with a mother whose first response on learning of the death of her grandson was, "Oh God, Brad, just what we need now, a death in the family. Not during the holidays!"

"Oh Jesus, mother," Thompson replied to himself, "you think this is some cruel joke played just for your benefit?"

Frustration that he was not in control of his own destiny, in the face of indifferent parents, an uncaring wife, and economic uncertainty.

Frustration that was about to boil into festering resentment. Over the next two years the energy from this resentment would propel Thompson into the national limelight as the Indiana Grand Dragon of the American Knights of the Ku Klux Klan, a group that *Klanwatch* of the Southern Poverty Law Center labels two years later as being "remarkable" for their "crude racism and threats." A group whose membership, according to *Klanwatch*, experienced "explosive" growth while Thompson was Grand Dragon, shooting from one chapter in Indiana in 1996 to twelve by the following year.

Festering resentment that led to a thirty minute (all-expenses paid) hate-filled appearance on the Jerry Springer show. Thompson's face on the front pages of two dozen newspapers from Indiana to Ohio to Michigan to Pennsylvania to West Virginia to North Carolina and South Carolina. Radio talk shows across the Midwest. Brad Thompson says this. Brad Thompson says that. The Klan is back. The Klan is here to stay. It's not against the law to be in the Klan. The Klan has free speech. The Klan is protecting your free speech. And to hell with anyone who tries to take it away.

Pure, unadulterated, festering resentment.

For resentment is the essence of the modern Klan. Resentment, as historian David Chalmers puts it in his 1981 revision of *Hooded Americanism*, against a society that fails to give any breaks, let alone any status, to the working class stiffs that make up the rank and file of the modern Klan. "Whatever his place in the class structure, the Klansman resents his lack of recognition and prestige in society," asserts Chalmers quite simply and convincingly.

Resentment that roiled over Thompson after his son's death in wave after wave. Resentment like what Abraham—a God-fearing, law-abiding man if there ever was one—must have felt, but dared not articulate, 4,000 years ago when God challenged him to sacrifice his own beloved son Isaac.

Resentment that the modern Klan spews in venomous tirades from the steps of antique courthouses across America's heartland. Resentment against blacks, Jews, "faggots"—any number of "special interest groups" Klan leaders claim are favored by the government and today's society over their own white membership.

Resentment Thompson felt—his life in ashes despite all his hard work to provide for his family—when the doctor told him, blocking his view into the emergency room, "We lost him."

"You lost what? What in the hell did you lose? How do you lose a kid in a hospital? Lose him? Lose him? What a horrible word. Just tell me my son is dead. Say it, say it, say it. Who in the hell do you think you are to tell me you 'lost' my son?" Thompson thought, staring in dumb disbelief at the helpless, fumbling doctor.

Thompson still chokes, the frustration and icy resentment return with a rush, when he remembers the night Bart died.

"Just another night at my machine. Another argument at home.

Another shitty night at work, staring at a boring, fucking machine," Thompson recalls.

"The phone calls don't surprise me no more. Leslie always has a problem. She couldn't care less that the Auburn Foundry is a huge place and sometimes I'm not terribly easy to find. So when my fore-man comes skittering around my machine with this worried look on his face and says I need to go to the hospital right away, I just figure maybe Bart's leg is broke again. Or maybe his arm," Thompson told me about a year after he quit the Klan.

"I didn't even hurry," Thompson remembers, with a hint of hor-ror now in his voice. "I took my own sweet-ass time. I can still see myself sitting in the parking lot, starting my car, thinking about what I'd find. Already resentful that I'd have to be lying to the nurses again. Lying to the welfare lady that it was just an accident. No one's fault. Certainly not Leslie's. So I didn't hurry. I wasn't wor-ried. In fact I was mad. Leslie again. More hysteria. More lies. I was pretty fucking sick of it all. I wasn't looking forward to facing the doctor, having to make up another bullshit story. My whole fucking life was a story."

But Thompson quits his pity trip when he arrives at the hospi-tal ahead of the ambulance.

"Something's wrong. Where's the ambulance? It should be here by now," he thinks.

"Auburn is a small town. The Foundry is five minutes from my trailer, and our trailer park is ten minutes from the hospital. So where's Leslie's car? Why isn't the ambulance parked here like it's been the other times? Why's it so quiet? This don't make no sense."

Thompson is the only one in the dark, though, for there is no reason to rush. The ambulance driver knows that. He pulls in with-out the siren blaring. Without urgently flashing strobe lights.

His unease now gives way to sharp dread. Something's clearly wrong. What does it mean that no one is in a hurry?

All too soon Thompson finds out the reason.

"We lost him."

After fifteen minutes of frustrating delay in the emergency room, the doctor utters the dreadful, meaningless words. Thompson is al-lowed to see his son—one last time. "If you think you can handle it," the doctor says.

He "handles" it by himself, as Leslie is already knocked out, in a spare bed in the emergency room, after an hysterical fit.

"Bart wasn't even cold yet. He was lying on his side, one cheek down on the gurney. I touched the other cheek, it was still warm. He could have been asleep," Thompson tells me, eyes even now bulging with held back tears, as he spreads out the death notices and sympathy cards on his coffee table, speaking slowly so as not to give away the tremble in his voice.

"Oh God, why Bart? It should be me lying here," Thompson said to himself at the time. "I was the good-for-nothing one. I was the one couldn't do nothing right. Bart didn't deserve this. He didn't do nothing wrong. He was stubborn, he was strong willed. He was bull-headed. But he didn't do nothing wrong."

To this day the details of Bart's death are a little sketchy. Other than that Thompson was at work as usual and that Leslie, at least by her account, was at home watching their two toddlers.

"I still don't know exactly how he died. Just that he choked to death right here in this living room, right there next to you by the fish tank. On a slice of bread. First he stopped breathing, then his heart stopped. Practically right where you're sitting," Thompson said, not looking at me but staring off into the distance at some private memory of grief.

"There's still times I feel like I'm walking in a dream, that I'm right there again looking at Bart on the gurney. I can still feel the warmth of his check," he adds, almost in a trance.

"Oh God. Oh Bart. God help me. God help Bart. This isn't right. This isn't fair. I know I'm a worthless piece of shit. But it's not right to take it out on Bart. Tell me he's just asleep. Dear God. This really sucks," he moans, burying his head in his hands as the memories of that terrible night, still fresh after more than three years, come flooding back.

So Thompson, already angry at himself, already angry at his wife, and now angry at the doctor for saying he'd "lost" his son just as if he had lost a set of car keys, is about to ascend to a new plateau of rage.

For there is no merciful God for Brad to relieve him of his burden after he has passed Abraham's ultimate test.

There is only the resentful anger, with more to come.

"It's unbelievable the shit you go through when someone in your family dies," he recalls with a trace of venom seeping into his voice. "And if it's a kid, it's just unbearable. It just never stops. Your grief is so terrible you know there's no fucking way you can possibly function. But you have no choice."

Thompson remembers those dreadful days before and after Thanksgiving—days in which he had little if anything to be thankful about—all too clearly

"Everybody wants something from you. You have a million decisions to make. And everybody's making a buck off of each of those decisions. Days and days are like this. I'm crying all the time. But I have to order a coffin. Only the finest will do for my son, but I can't afford it. You have to have a plot. You have to have a hole. A headstone. A church. A preacher. One decision after another, and everyone holding out their hand for a buck."

At first Thompson was consumed by grief. He was grieving too hard to be angry. But it wasn't long before it was anger that was eating him up.

"I got pretty fucking angry pretty damn quick. Angry at everyone wanting me to pay something, something for this, something for that, on account of my son being dead."

Thompson had to borrow money—$3,000—to cover the funeral expenses. At eighteen percent interest. And even that wasn't enough, but fortunately his friends at the foundry chipped in to pay for Bart's headstone.

"I was pretty humiliated. The funeral people—they assumed I was trailer trash—and when they delivered Bart to the church, they asked right there, on the spot, for their money. I couldn't believe it. Right in front of all the mourners. Right in front of the family. He wasn't even in the ground yet."

That angered Thompson.

"Cold and bitter. That was me. These sons of bitches only doing this for the money."

Putting Bart in the ground did nothing to bury Thompson's anger.

In fact, over the dark months of winter his anger grew, as he realized Leslie didn't share his grief—let alone his bed anymore. And it wasn't long before he learned that nights he left Leslie home alone with Joey while he went off to work, Leslie wasn't alone at all. Not at all.

"You could say this wasn't a very good time for me. I was in a rage all the time. I was feeling so hateful, it occurred to me more than once that maybe I wanted to shoot someone. Some of my buddies at the foundry suggested that where they'd come from—Kentucky and West Virginia—that a real man would've shot some one long time ago. My wife. Her boyfriend. It didn't make no difference," Thompson said. "Those old hillbillies were good people, but they had their own strong sense of justice."

Thompson thought about his friends' advice a lot. No, not a lot—all the time.

Police checkpoint, LaGrange, Indiana, 1996

"I played those tapes over and over constantly in my head. Bart looking asleep. The doctor who 'lost' my son. The moneygrubbers at the funeral parlor. Leslie and what I found at my home, behind my back, while I was working twelve hours a day, six days a week," he remembers nearly four years later, eyes narrowing still at the thought of the outrage. "I could've shot the lot of them," he freely admits.

But Thompson was too worn out to act on his impulse.

He threw himself into his work. Haunted by the greedy glint in the bankers' and undertakers' eyes, he vowed never to have an empty bank account again. He drove himself at the foundry, accepting every hour they would send his way.

"All I did was work. I came home. Slept. And went back to work. I never even took no time to eat. I lost a lot of weight during that time," he recalls.

And he also lost Leslie.

Good riddance, he finally realized, because he gained Joey in the ensuing custody battle when his first wife Brenda offered to help him out of his misery by agreeing to remarry him on the spot and move back into the trailer to watch the little boy.

And another old friend—one Thompson didn't even know he had—came forth with some good advice.

"I didn't even like this guy," Thompson recalls with a hint of

Jeff and Edna Berry

shame. "But he knew me, and one day he came up to me at the foundry and said my friends there were just shooting me a lot of bad shit. That they were just fueling my rage and that if I went on like this, all hateful all the time and everything, I'd wind up dead or in prison. He said I really needed to quit dwelling on my hate, that I needed to let go of Bart and Leslie and find something else to do with my life."

Good advice, but poor timing, for in a parallel universe only eleven miles away in Newville, Indiana, an equally frustrated, aging Klansman is busily reinventing himself.

A former informant for the Dekalb County prosecutor's office while working off probation for a handful of petty crimes including larceny and fraud, self-employed mechanic Jeff Berry has discovered there are a few bucks to be made in the Klan. Always a shrewd survivor, he's figured out that wearing a blue and gold robe and shouting at a crowd on a Saturday afternoon sure beats the heck out of changing oil and pulling blown cylinder heads.

Berry, forty-two at the time, whose brash ways keep him just one step out of the slammer, has recently declared himself "Imperial Wizard" of the "American Knights" of the Ku Klux Klan.

"I didn't know nothing about him at the time, although Newville is just twenty minutes east of here, but I was starting to hear something about a new Klan in Indiana," said Thompson. "The media was talking about a big rally coming up in Angola and showing a lot of old films on the old Indiana Klan from the 1920's. I was pretty fascinated. The media was too. There hadn't been nothing about the Klan here for years and years—no one could remember when. Then suddenly Jeff Berry's name's on TV and in all the newspapers. It's like some big mysterious deal come back to life out of our dim past. A real live, Imperial Wizard right here, in our own time."

Thompson was impressed. "It was like I was living just a few miles away from a legend that had suddenly true," he told me, eyes animated at his recollection of his first contact with the Klan.

Always a big reader of popular history—his bookshelf that seems to hold up one wall of his aging trailer is crammed with accounts of WWII—Thompson was particularly fascinated with the historical aspects of the Klan.

"I started reading up on it. On the old Klan. I'm not sure why. Something to take my mind off Bart and Leslie. Something where my hate and rage ain't quite so empty. Something I can focus on. Sink my teeth into."

Thompson was surprised about what he learned. Klansmen, at least historically, weren't all hillbillies and white trash, as he had supposed at first. Some—particularly in the 1920's when for almost a full decade it was socially acceptable, even preferable in many circles, to be in the Klan—were quite shrewd. Many, he discovered, were state legislators and civic leaders. One prominent member, President Warren Harding, even took the Klan oath in the oval office, according to sociologists Betty Dobratz and Stephanie Shanks-

Meile. Another, Hugo Black, was a Supreme Court Justice. Others, like Indiana Grand Dragon D. C. Stephenson, pulled political strings in cigar-filled cloakrooms, working behind the scenes to amass both great power and great wealth.

And Indiana was then right at the epicenter of the national Klan movement.

Leonard Moore, in his landmark book, *Citizen Klansmen*, estimated that five million men and women joined the Klan in the 1920's. He reports that Indiana between 1921 and 1928 was home to "the largest and most politically powerful state Klan organization of the era."

This appealed to Thompson.

"Like these people in this state used to really have their shit together. D. C. Stephenson, he was a millionaire right here in Indiana. They hated Catholics and immigrants here, and Stephenson got a dollar off of every Klansman he recruited, every year, so pretty soon he was rich and all the politicians was afraid of him. His Klan was so big, that he could get the governor of Indiana to do what he told him to. They wasn't afraid of nobody, and if the Indiana Klan said jump, everybody jumped."

So Thompson told Brenda they ought to check out the upcoming rally in nearby Angola. It could be a piece of history they might never see again.

"Angola's just up the road. It couldn't hurt us none and it might be fun. In the old days, in the 1920's in Indiana, Klan rallies was like circuses, or carnivals. They was these giant family picnics. There'd be thousands of people there, like in Kokomo or Muncie. Big parades, with horses, everyone in their robes and hoods and then a giant hog roast afterwards. In them days Klan rallies was family fun," he was thinking.

"I wasn't thinking of it as some kind of anti-black thing. Hell, I grew up in a Midwestern town—Pioneer, Ohio—where we didn't even have no blacks. And Auburn don't have many. The ones where I work—they did their job and I did mine. It wasn't no big deal. Blacks, Muslims, we have them all at the Foundry. I never paid no attention. I was busy working. So were they. I never thought about it—about their color or nationality or whatever—until later," Thompson recalls.

"Frankly I think I was just looking for something different to do. Something to get my mind out of its rut. Something maybe a little scary, a little different, a little thrilling. Like a Klan rally's not your every day sort of event you know? It's more like something jumping out at you from the darker pages of history."

Thompson doesn't know it yet, but his reasons for going to Jeff Berry's Angola rally are about to turn him into a textbook example of a Klansman. A perfect profile. A predictable fit.

"This is so typical," observes writer Patsy Sims, whose 1978 book *the Klan* stepped for the first time outside of history and musty newspaper accounts to record the living thoughts of nearly 100 active Klansmen of that period across the deep South and Appalachia.

"I saw it time and time again. These are people from drab and dreary communities, with monotonous lives, with low self-esteem, who are looking for something that will make them feel differently about themselves," she told me well after Brad Thompson ran his brutal course as Indiana Grand Dragon.

"These are people who have very mundane lives, with menial jobs, living in fairly modest, rundown homes. Being in the Klan is a way to help them escape having to face this," she added.

She laughed when I told her that Indiana's most recent Grand Dragon had admitted to me he had lived his entire life with little if any contact with the people he professed to hate.

"It's not at all uncommon that they don't know any blacks. Some of the most virulent racists I met came from all-white communities. That's why they could be the way they were—they simply didn't know any better. That's not an excuse, it's just a statement of fact."

And Thompson, even before his first rally, fit the profile in one other way—a way that makes a Klan rally a very strong magnet well beyond its racist implications. His comment to me that he thought the Angola rally might be "a little scary," yet he planned to go anyhow, struck a cord that resonates, apparently, among many would-be Klansmen.

Months before I asked Thompson about his thinking that brought him to his first rally, I attended a Klan party and cross burning at Jeff Berry's home in Newville, Indiana, where I met Robert Moore.

Moore, despite his full beard and heavily tattooed arms sporting Klan symbols and marijuana leaves, is a soft spoken man with a luscious North Carolina drawl. At the time I knew little about him, other than his rank as Exalted Cyclops of the American Knights for the Asheville area. Later I learned he was the same Robert Moore identified by the *Intelligence Report* of the Southern Poverty Law

Robert Moore

Center as the Klansman who threatened to "massacre" counter-demonstrators if they dared oppose his forthcoming rally in Asheville.

Anxious to talk to me and explain in his quiet way his feelings of unfairness and victimization at the hands of the larger society, he did not seem at all like the hooded Klansman who, according to the SPLC's winter 1997 issue of *Intelligence Report*, told the Asheville press a year earlier, "We're coming there to have a peaceful assembly..., but they throw one rock, it won't take us but eighty-eight seconds to wipe out what's standing across the street, and God forbid if there's any children there."

(To be fair, sociologists Betty Dobratz and Stephanie Shanks-Meile found that watchdog groups like the Southern Poverty Law Center occasionally overstated their claims. "For instance, events were sometimes portrayed in *Klanwatch Intelligence Reports* as more militant and dangerous with higher turnouts than we observed," they wrote in their introduction to *White Power, White Pride!*)

But back to his own attendance at his first rally, near Greenville, North Carolina, Moore recalled to me that he wasn't keen on the idea at the time. "My friends said we ought to do it, but I told them the Klan was a bunch of crazy, scary fuckers. I was scared, and I didn't mind admitting it."

But he went anyway. In spite of the fear. Or more likely because of the fear. Historian David Chalmers identifies this subliminal attraction the Klan poses for young, white males as "the cherished possibility" of "rough stuff."

And once there, just as Thompson would discover in Angola, he was hooked.

Chapter Two:
The View from the Courthouse Steps

Butler Courthouse, March 1998

The road to Angola was a perilous one. For the Angola rally turned out to be the point of no return.

But Thompson did not feel the impending doom. He did not glimpse the onrushing nightmare. He only smelled excitement in the air. A sense of adventure. A little walk on the wild side—the promise of that cherished "rough stuff" spoken of by historian David Chalmers.

But his wife Brenda, though always dutiful (especially with her second chance of keeping her man), was a reluctant voyager. "Why did I want to go see a bunch of fucking—what did that John Grisham fellow call them in his novel—Kluckers, I think. I already knew enough rednecks," she told me a year after disaster crashed around Thompson's head, sending him in to an AA and antabuse program so that he could keep his job, let alone hold onto his wife and young son.

"I asked Brad if he really knew what he was doing, but me, dumb me, I agreed to go along anyhow," Brenda remembered.

"To keep the peace," she added.

"We was tired of arguing about it, so we just finally jumped in the car and didn't say a word the whole way up. I think we was nervous," Thompson recalls.

Thompson's first fear was that he would be spotted by someone he knew, like someone from work. Or that the media would be there and he'd accidentally get his face on TV and that his parents might be watching the news that night—worries that were well-founded—with a lot of heckling and ridicule awaiting him at the foundry the following Monday. And not to mention an icy silence from his mom and dad, who caught the TV broadcast of the rally with their son on the "supporter" side of the police lines.

"That worried me a lot, when I saw that the cops were stopping the crowd and making them declare if they was for or against, before they'd let them into separate areas to get close enough to the Klan to really see and hear."

Thompson explained that the local police, with the help of state police Klan experts, had devised a way to keep the protestors and the sympathizers away from each other, after a serious battle among spectators the year before when a different faction of the Klan staged a rally in Indianapolis.

"I wasn't sure what I was going to say, right up until I got to the barricade, but since I wasn't really against 'em, I said I was a supporter and went on into the fenced area with the other supporters. I was really worried who was going to see me, yet since I didn't know what else to say, there I was."

But Thompson wasn't the least bit worried that he'd be recruited by the Klan that day.

"It absolutely never occurred to me that I'd be joining the Klan. That was the furthest thing from my mind. I was going to the rally strictly out of curiosity, out of wanting to get a little look at history for myself," he reported.

However, once within ear-shot of Jeff Berry's patented tirade,

Thompson found himself mesmerized.

By the sound and the fury.

By the pseudo pomp and circumstance.

By the seductive rhetoric of easy solutions to complex problems.

Jeff and Edna Berry, Butler, 1998

"Like these people weren't entirely the dumb hillbillies I thought they was going to be. Some of the stuff ole Jeff was saying up there in his blue robe actually made some sense."

Thompson was struck, indeed, by what he saw and heard that day.

Angola is by any standard your typical Midwestern county seat.

It's not at all unlike Butler, Pennsylvania, where three years later and a full 12 months after Thompson had fallen from the Klan's grace, Jeff Berry was still reveling in pushing the state police around and in rousing a lazy Saturday afternoon crowd turned out for some cheap entertainment.

Like a rock group taking the stage, twenty-five mostly hooded and masked members of the American Knights of the Ku Klux Klan strut up the courthouse steps in this rural Pennsylvania town a short, scenic drive north of Pittsburgh. It's a promising spring day in late March of 1998. The rasping roar of blaring rock music by the likes of Bruce Springsteen, Ted Nugent, and other patriotic rockers heralds the Klan's colorful entrance. Standing tall and proud in their outlandish garb, this self selected and earnest group of social outcasts is greeted by the cheers and jeers of a lily-white crowd of some 600 supporters, protestors, and just plain old-fashioned, curious citizens from this steelmaking town of 100,000 souls in the western foothills of the Appalachian Mountains.

"So what's the difference between the white robes and the black robes?" asks one bystander, a businessman, with his long sleeve dress shirt and collar open where he loosened his tie after closing up shop for the afternoon. "I'm just here," he quickly explains, "because we all agreed to close our businesses for the afternoon, and I'm just curious as to what these people are all about." The local newspaper, the *Butler Eagle*, reported that the downtown merchants association voted to shut down Saturday afternoon, as a message to the Klan.

"We want to say to the KKK and their supporters that we don't want their business," Mary McCorry, president of Butler's downtown merchants' group, told *the Eagle*. "They're not welcome here."

So just what is the Klan's business here on a warm, sunny, early spring afternoon?

Surrounded by orange security fence and an array of some 100 city, county and state police, safe from the noisy protestors who ardently heckled the group during their ninety minutes of speeches and music, the Klan is here for a variety of reasons. Some of those reasons are openly acknowledged and some are more subtle.

On one level, the Klan is here today to put on a good show. The few that don't wear hoods and masks are clearly basking in the warm sunlight. They are clearly enjoying both the cheers and jeers of the crowd. With their Confederate and American flags brilliantly waving in the steady breeze, they are clearly reveling in the pomp and pageantry of their own shining costumes and colorful regalia.

Jeff Berry, the Imperial Wizard of the American Knights, is adorned today in a sparkling blue robe with gold cape and piping.

Edna, his wife of twenty-five years, whom he introduces to the cheering crowd as the Imperial Wizard of the Ladies Auxiliary, is decked out in reverse, with a gold robe, blue cape and blue piping. Neither wear hoods. Their faces betray little anxiety or dismay, even when the protestors near-constant chant of "fuck the Klan" drowns out their message. In fact, the louder the protestors, the more animated become their expressions.

Many of the Klansmen are dressed, of course, in traditional white robes. Those with orange piping on their sleeves hold the rank of Exalted Cyclops—a rank much like being the county chairman of a political party. In the white robes with green piping, are the Grand

Nighthawk, Butler Rally

Dragons. Present for today's rally are the new Indiana Grand Dragon and the Pennsylvania Grand Dragon. They represent the top Klan leadership in each state and answer directly to the Imperial Wizard.

Other Klansmen are dressed in flowing black robes with red piping. These are the Nighthawks, the security force of the Klan. Today they have been thoroughly frisked by the state police and are not armed. But at private Klan functions they are often heavily and openly armed, guarding against surprise intrusion. "We do not believe in violence," blares one Klansman into the overamplified microphone during the rally, "but we will protect ourselves."

Klan protestor, Butler, 1998

Those not robed are Klan members, but they have not yet been "naturalized." Some of the newcomers wear masks, much like the Zapatista rebels of Chiapas, Mexico, to protect their identities.

From the Klan's point of view, they are here today as a public service.

Although they will get to it soon enough, they do not open with their traditional messages of bigotry and separatism.

The Pennsylvania Grand Dragon takes the microphone first, after their opening rock anthem has been turned off, to announce that the American Knights of the Ku Klux Klan have posted a $500 reward for the name of the person who torched a nearby church several months before.

"We want to know who this person is. We will deal with him

ourselves, and then we will turn him over to the authorities," exclaims the Grand Dragon, urging people to call the Klan's Pennsylvania number, or failing that to call the Bureau of Alcohol, Tobacco and Firearm hotline, which he incorrectly identifies as 1-800-ATF-FIRE.

The church burning, however, is not today's main agenda. The American Knights like to say they have been "called into" a commu-

Klan Protestors, Butler, 1998

nity by residents who are concerned about some issue of freedom or fairness. At a 1996 rally in LaGrange, Indiana, home to many Amish who have escaped Pennsylvania's crowded and touristy conditions to take up farming in a quieter environment, the issue allegedly was the death of a young Amish girl killed in a farming accident. The Klan claimed that this untimely death, which went unprosecuted, illustrated the special status afforded to the Amish at the expense of the general population. In Cicero, Illinois, two years later, where their planned rally was aborted at the last minute after the town brokered a payment of $10,000 from a private citizen to distribute Klan literature in lieu of a disruptive appearance by the Klan, the issue, at least in theory, was police corruption. The Klan charged that Cicero police allegedly turned a blind eye to drug dealing there by the black population from nearby Chicago. (I've heard this baseless charge of "police corruption" used as the "reason" many times over for the Klan's appearance in a community.)

Today's rally had a similar "noble" theme for the Klan to harp on: an allegedly overcrowded juvenile detention center in nearby

Jeff Berry (center) on the LaGrange courthouse steps

Herman, a quiet suburb amidst the beautiful hills overlooking Butler.

"We have been called here today, because residents of your community want our help," shouts the Pennsylvania Grand Dragon. Describing the overcrowding of the facility and its alleged lack of security, with what he claimed was a consequential decline in property values and in enrollment at a nearby Catholic school, he continues. "We of the American Knights do not know of how many blacks there are in this facility. We don't care. We don't care. What we do know is this facility has seriously destructed the community of Herman, and it must close!"

Closing his statement to great cheers from many of the spectators, his voice soars above the crowd. "The government is supposed to be of the people, by the people and for the people. So we demand that this facility be closed now! Release the residents of this beautiful community of Herman from their fear! Thank you!"

Speaking next, to more cheering, is Jeff Berry, the Imperial Wizard of the American Knights. "We are the people. You are the people. Take a stand!" he begins. "Join the Klan, stick up for your rights!"

Berry, a shrewd man who is quite pleasant one on one to the point of appearing downright reasonable, is a different person when he dons the purple trappings of his office and stands on the courthouse steps—well-guarded by police—before a shouting mob.

Quickly casting aside any pretense of civility, Berry launches into a screed against the federal income tax, which he tells the audience goes to support the "mud race." Ratcheting up the volume, he screams out, "Only God has the right to create a race—not no black and white, not no nigger, not no Jew."

This, what ever it means, rouses the crowd, and Berry shouts over the din, "Yes, I will use the word *nigger*, because it is not illegal!"

Really wound up now, Berry screeches into the microphone his patented definition of the word *nigger*—"a dirty low-down scum who takes from society."

Now the crowd is frenzied, with the protestors jumping up and down shooting birds at the Klan. Their supporters jump up and down, too, middle fingers raised to the protestors.

"We are sick and tired of the government taking your money, and giving food and jobs to the niggers when the white race has to go without! Wake up America," Berry shrieks.

At this point one bystander, a grandmotherly white woman, seeing my tape recorder, leans over and says to me, "They can flush that kind of talk down the toilet as far as I'm concerned." Her friend chimes in, "*the Eagle* can put this on the obit page, and even that would be too much reporting."

Pausing for a bit more rock and roll, Berry passes the microphone to another speaker, who rouses the crowd with choice remarks about "race mixing" and homosexuals. Says another bystander into my tape recorder, "These speakers are awful."

But at the same time one nearby teenaged white woman is jumping up and down screaming, "I'm white and proud of it!"

Time now for a little parading, as Berry and his wife take their American and Confederate flags and strut up and down the cordoned-off street separating the courthouse steps from the crowd, waving their banners to the blast of more deafening rock music.

After this brief respite, Berry climbs back to the top of the court-house steps and blares into the microphone. "God made Adam and Eve—not Adam and Steve. I am sick and tired of all this talk about same sex marriage, there is no such thing," he screams to a great angry roar from the crowd.

Then pointing to an enraged young man in the crowd of protest-ors, heavily tattooed and with many pierced rings in his lips and ears, Berry yells out, "Same sex marriages give us idiots like that man standing over there who don't know what the hell they are.

A little "rough stuff"

Some one needs to take a hammer and bust him up against the side of the head."

Berry is pressing his luck with statements like that. I've seen rock concerts in Indiana closed down for less threatening remarks than that. But the Butler authorities are patient, waiting to see if Berry will take enough verbal rope to hang himself—he has been arrested before for incitement to riot.

At this point, though, the police move in closer to the man in question, pointedly giving dirty looks to anyone who makes a move in his direction.

But Berry keeps right up, launching next into an attack on the churches. "I am sick and tired of this. You've got all these churches around here that say this is okay, but the only reason they say it is okay is so that all these homosexual fagots will come to their church and put money in their pot! So they can turn around and buy candy bars to molest the little boys that go to their church. That is called economics."

Realizing he's sort of lost the crowd at this point, which is momentarily a little subdued as it tries to follow his reasoning, Berry changes tactics and starts hollering, "Take a stand, join the Klan. Take a stand, join the Klan. It is not against the law to be in the Klan!"

At this point the protestors drown him out, chanting with great

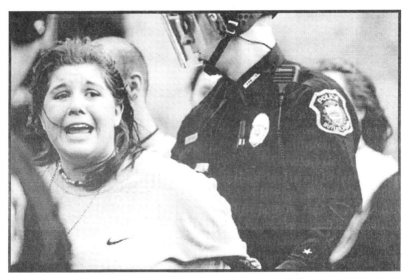

Butler Klan supporter on her way to jail

volume over and over, "Suck my dick. Suck my dick."

Berry shouts back, "You dirty pieces of shit," and tempers flare to the point some spectators trade blows and the police make their first arrest of the day.

The rally at this point has degenerated into a shouting match. The voices of the Klan and their supporters are completely drowned out by a group of young white people, collegiate looking in their neat T-shirts and khaki shorts, rapidly chanting over and over and over, "Fuck you, fuck you, fuck you."

This, of course, gives the Klan great satisfaction, and they in turn drown out the protestors by cranking up the rock music and parading once more up and down the street with their waving flags.

"Just don't forget we're here defending your free speech," Berry taunts the protestors.

"Take a stand, join the Klan, America. This is your country, take it back, take it back by any means necessary," he adds at full volume.

Berry, who speaks extemporaneously, after uttering this suggestive threat launches into a tirade about language. "Eubonics, bubonics, what kind of shit is that? Speak English or get the hell out of America," he demands, his voice rising to a crescendo.

"White trash," responds one protestor into a momentary lull of the histrionics, to which Berry retorts, "That's right, that's exactly what you are."

The Klan enjoys these outbursts from the protestors, because it gives them a chance to strike back. One Klansman takes the microphone and shouts at the protestors who at this point are yelling again at the supporters, "That just shows how dumb you niggers and nigger lovers are (even though there are but three blacks in the crowd, all young women) because you are outnumbered twenty to one!" (The Associated Press estimated this crowd at 600 strong, with perhaps one-third of that there because they supported the Klan.)

By now, after an hour of shouting in the sun, the rally is degenerating into random name calling, with no central theme to the Klan's message, beyond the basic message of racial hatred. "When are you young men finally going to take a stand and take back your white women from these damn niggers," shouts one Klansmen, absolutely apropos of nothing, as Butler, if not a white-only town, is certainly tacitly segregated socially. In a full morning spent at the town's big, prosperous mall on the north side, I saw only a handful of blacks.

Still taunting the white protestors, the Klansman rambles on. "All you little nigger boys out there," he shouts pointing at the collegiate group of noisemakers, "All you little nigger boys, you are nothing but worthless pieces of shit in my book."

Emboldened by this line of reasoning—as puzzled as the crowd appears by now—a Klansman who identifies himself as the Exalted Cyclops from Cambridge, Ohio, declares into the microphone, "I'm tired of all this affirmative action. Miss Nigger America. The United Nigger College Fund. Nigger Entertainment Television. These are all a slap in the face of white people. What do you think would happen if there was anything public for white people only?"

This now, is the red meat of a Klan rally, and the audience is finally listening attentively.

"That's right. This is discrimination against white people, and the Ku Klux Klan is fighting to put an end to this discrimination. Enough is enough already. This generation didn't do anything wrong and we are tired of being punished, for nothing. We did not bring the nigger from Africa, and we certainly are not keeping him here. They were brought here by Jews and their own people. We want nothing to do with the American nigger and his animalistic ways."

Speaking from his notes, this Klansman sums up the whole point of this rally, and others like it: Klansmen, in their minds, are the final barrier, the last hope against an onslaught of darkness.

"If you are born in America, you are an American, not African-American. The Ku Klux Klan is the only organization in the United States that has enough guts to stand up for true decency. As white Christian Americans, the Ku Klux Klan may be America's only salvation. Anyone who is against the Klan is against America."

He punctuates this thought with "White Power!" That refrain is reflected back across the courthouse steps to a roaring response from the crowd. Klan supporters cheer and yell "White Power" in return. The protestors follow with a deafening, rolling, chant: "Klan go home, Klan go home!"

Pretty soon the protestors and supporters are jeering each other again, and the police step in and make more arrests when two young men fall to blows. A few others who are overly belligerent are chased away from the security fence, back into the anonymity of the crowd.

This crowd, as with those at many other Klan rallies across the Midwest, is predominately young and very white. The youngest— high school and college students—clutch to the security fence and hurl epithets at the Klan and shoot birds. Vocal Klan supporters, also generally young, spend a lot of time at the security fence jumping up and down and yelling "White power" or "White and proud of it."

But not all Klan supporters get near the center of the activity. Some hang back and seek out the press. One young woman, a petite mother of four who said she was a professional floral designer, challenged me to put her views in these pages. "You're only interested in the people who make good photographs and are causing trouble, aren't you? Hate sells, right?" she said of the protestors who were shooting birds at the Klan.

She said she supported the Klan because she liked their message about decency. "There's a lot of stuff coming into the schools, into our homes, that's just not right these days. But we can't do anything about it. The schools can't discipline our kids, and we don't dare either. Somebody has to say something about this."

That somebody, in her mind, is the Klan.

An older man, who identified himself as a seventy-five year old grandfather, said the churches had gotten too liberal. He liked the Klan's message about what's wrong with today's churches. "It's not a race thing, it's about discipline. That's what I like," he said.

But one young man, heavily ear-ringed, and sporting a tongue stud, wandered over to this conversation and said he didn't feel that way at all. "I've learned finally that you've got to live with people of all kinds. We all have to live together— I don't see any choice but to get along. That doesn't mean I'd marry outside of my race, 'cause you see what it does to the kids, they're lost, but I don't know...," he drifted off.

One middle-aged woman, however, had a different approach. Running with her daughter in tow to the back of the courthouse where she knew the Klan would be disrobing for their bus ride back to their cars, she whipped out her pocket camera and started taking pictures of the unhooded Klansmen and their supporters. "I just want to look at these pictures and see if I recognize anyone. I'll make sure my friends know who these people are, and we won't patronize where they work or have anything to do with them."

But Berry, the Imperial Wizard, and his two bodyguards from Indiana aren't fazed by having their pictures taken with their hoods off, as they never wear hoods. "It's not illegal to be in the Klan," he likes to note.

Chapter Three:
The Imperial Wizard as Civil Libertarian

Mike McQueeney, Jeff Berry, Robert Moore, Edna Berry and Tonya Berry
around the kitchen table at the Berry home in Newville, Indiana

I t's not illegal to be in the Klan—a favorite refrain of the American Knights as they spew their venomous spiel across the courthouse steps of the Midwest.

It's this tough-talking, simple logic, that captured the imagination of Brad Thompson.

"Like I was totally amazed. I was expecting some tobacco chewing, toothless hillbillies, and here I find instead some people that was actually talking some sense," Thompson recalls thinking after the Angola rally.

"Ole Jeff, con artist or not, has a way with words. He's not afraid to be blunt, to come right out and say what others are only half thinking," Thompson observes.

So just what kind of guy is this self-proclaimed Imperial Wizard of the American Knights of the Ku Klux Klan?

Brash, for sure. Self-confidant, certainly. Going head to head with a judge in Cicero, Illinois, or the mayor of Huntington, West Virginia, is all in a day's work for this rough-hewn mechanic turned civil libertarian.

Shrewd and crafty too.

"He knows how to make a buck. That's all the Klan is to him," asserts Thompson.

But there's more than that.

"He'd do anything for a friend. That's what's hurt me the most about getting out of the Klan—losing Jeff's friendship," Thompson reports with real remorse. "He was a real family man too. Very protective of his wife and kids, and of his friends too. When you was one of Jeff Berry's friends, you really had something going for yourself."

But what's this overtly racist and homophobic man really like, up close and personal, on a "day off," without his flashy robe and armed body guards. Just what drew the likes of Brad Thompson and others into this headlong race of modern madness that propels his small band of merry men and women from courthouse to courthouse, from angry mob to angry mob, on Saturday afternoons when much of the rest of America is absorbed by golf or college football?

Who is Jeff Berry?

Try this for starters: a March afternoon on the first warm Sunday of 1998. I knock on his door (his back door), and enter the neat kitchen of the Berry family, where Jeff is seated at his kitchen table busily engaged on the telephone. Two other men—neighbors, not Klansmen—idly stir their coffee waiting for Jeff to get the caller—who dialed in on the Klan line (equipped with caller ID)—off the phone.

The interview begins before I can even get my notepad out of my pocket. Putting down the phone with an exasperated shake of his head, Berry looks me right in the eye with barely a hello and says, "We don't take no Nazis."

And don't even think of calling 219-337-KKKK to talk some trash. "These guys that call and say they want to join the Klan to kill some niggers, I just give them the phone number of another Klan."

The Imperial Wizard of the American Knights of the Ku Klux Klan, big hands wrapped warmly around a steaming coffee mug, is completely at ease. He's king of his castle in his knotty pine paneled home in Newville, Indiana, a hamlet literally a stone's throw from the Ohio state line.

He finishes talking hitches, gross vehicle weights and goose neck trailers with neighbors come a calling on a rainy Sunday afternoon and heads for the coffee pot. "What do you take in your coffee?" he asks affably.

"Black is fine," I respond, "it keeps my motor running no matter how it tastes." (Only now do I wonder if I've inadvertently made some sort of horrible Freudian pun, because normally I take milk in my coffee.)

One of the things that strikes you first about the "Reverend" Berry, as his business card claims him to be, is that he is not an enigma. You get what you see, and he's the first to admit it. Clad in his black Klan T-shirt, feet bare and cigarette dangling, this power-fully built man with slightly amused and very direct blue eyes behind his beard says, "You know me well enough by now—if I'm thinking it, I say it."

Completely comfortable talking about his politically incorrect views, as well he should be since he claims he has been a devoted Klansman for twenty-four years, Berry leans across the oval table in his kitchen—a kitchen as neat as a pin like the rest of his modest but comfortable home which he and his wife built practically with their bare hands—and calmly defines what he means by the word *nigger*.

"Our opinion of a nigger, no matter what color they are, is a dirty, lowdown person who takes and takes and takes from society and does not give anything back," he says in a throaty voice. "So therefore, my definition of a nigger shouldn't offend somebody because of their color."

And in fact, on this 1998 Sunday afternoon near the end of winter, Berry isn't interested in offending anyone. Happy to talk shop with neighbors who come calling to borrow his welding torches or who call on the phone to seek advice about a cracked cylinder block, he has the air of a man completely secure in his world. Capable of relaxing today with his wife Edna in their tastefully decorated home which neither hides nor boasts of their Klan status—a plaster bust and torso of a hooded Klansman resting on a corner of the living

Jeff Berry and police protection

room rug next to their well-equipped electronic entertainment center is the only obvious talisman of Berry's status as Imperial Wizard—Berry is completely pleasant with this reporter. If he remembers my 1996 vitriolic feature piece lambasting his group for the Klan's vicious verbal attacks on the nearby Amish communities that first drew the American Knight's attention to me, he hides it well.

"All we are interested in is the truth," says Berry's wife Edna. "You write your book and tell about us as we are. That's all we ask."

The Berrys as they are, and as they would be the first to admit, defy easy description.

Capable of spending a Sunday afternoon pleasantly drinking coffee with company they'd have every reason to show suspicion and hostility towards, they are equally as capable of looking forward, even talking openly of their anticipation, to next weekend's rally in Cicero, Illinois, where they have been told by the civic authorities there to expect gang violence to spill over from inner-city Chicago. This apparently bothers them not a whit, even though Edna has been injured at a rally before, by stone throwing protestors.

"Come here, look at this," Berry says as I try to head out the door after two exhausting hours of probing what makes these people seemingly at the fringe of American society tick like any other person. Berry hits the play button on the video player. A graphic tape— the Klan is adept at videotaping their own rallies—shows some startling images from a rally the year before in Ann Arbor, Michigan. At first the only sound on the tape is distant music and some noise from the crowd. The Klan is on the courthouse steps, still getting organized, but no one has started their speeches. The video camera scans the crowd. Suddenly breaking the silence near the camera is a distinct "thwack," then the images rushing into the camera lens are tilted close-ups of the courthouse steps, a door sill, linoleum floor inside a hall, then a woman on the floor, white robe absolutely drenched brilliant red, with a profusely bleeding head wound.

"That's Edna. She was hit by a stone. We hadn't even started talking. Now who do you call violent? What about our free speech?"

Free speech. There's the rub.

Berry maintains there are different kinds of Klans. The University of Illinois at Chicago Criminal Justice Institute lists more than a dozen unaffiliated Klan groups presently in the United States and Britain. The Southern Poverty Law Center breaks the count down even further than that, listing fifty-one separate Klan entities with 127 chapters active in 1997 across the United States. The American Knights—claimed by Berry to be the largest in the nation, with membership in thirty-eight states, plus a few in England and Iceland thanks to the Internet, which carries a web site with their registration form on it— is more of a civil rights group than a hate group, eschewing violence, he asserts.

"There's sitting out there, you know, different Klans. Different Klans have different views, okay? Even in my organization, there's a few people in my organization, if they see a black person—that is a nigger. There is hate. There is hate in their heart, okay?"

Berry says he doesn't see it quite that way himself.

"Me, if I see a black person, my theory is, my Mom always taught me, do not judge a book by its cover."

For example, Berry speaks almost reverently of the Honorable

Ellis Reid, circuit court judge for Cook County, where Berry testified the week before in a lawsuit to force the town of Cicero, Illinois, to halt its effort to prevent the Klan from holding a "political rally" there in March of 1998. "Now this is one of the finest men I've ever met. Now he is black, but he's no nigger." Of course it didn't hurt Berry's opinion of Judge Reid that he ruled in favor of the Klan's rights of free speech and freedom of assembly.

Berry maintains he is colorblind. It's a question of how he is treated by that other person, how that other person acts, he main-

Spectators and police, LaGrange, 1996

tains.

"I'm going to talk to you, if you are talking decent to me. You are a human being no matter what color you are. But if you start calling me an *MF* (Berry, at least in the privacy of his own home, is not given to vulgar language—that's what he said, "*MF*"), saying I'm going to kill you, your issues are bullshit, stuff like what I get on the phone all the time, 'cause my number is nationwide. So I tell them to hold up, do you actually know what the Klan stands for? Then if they respond, oh you *F*-ing cracker, I ask them if they know what a cracker is. Invariably they respond, 'No, you honky, what is it?'"

"So I say before you call someone a name, you'd better know what it means."

So just what does the Klan mean?

Brad Thompson, Berry's former Grand Dragon for Indiana, says it's little more than an economic scam for the people at the top.

"It's all about money and greed. Money and greed," Thompson claims to this day. "Rallies are nothing but membership drives, and Berry keeps the dues. He also sells T-shirts, souvenirs, pictures, videos, and he leases you the robes, for $85 each, and if you leave the Klan he takes your robe back and resells it. There's a lot of money changing hands," Thompson convincingly asserts.

Just look at the numbers.

"After we got nationwide publicity on the Jerry Springer show, we got hundreds and hundreds and hundreds of phone calls. People wanting to sign up, people wanting to send us their money. It took two of us manning the phones all day long, days and days in a row," recalls Thompson.

If that's the case, I ask, then where are these Kluckers when at most Berry can drag twenty-five or thirty robed members to a rally?

"That's not why most people join," responded Thompson. "It's a lot of work to participate in a rally. Most join just so they can have a card. A membership card to impress their girl friends or their drinking buddies."

Berry is disdainful of that analysis (but he won't report membership numbers, claiming it is a competitive secret).

"Yeah, my $250,000 home, my brand new pickup truck?" Berry responds with an expansive wave of his hand. "Edna and me, we built this house, her and me, ourselves. We lived on this property and then when they shot our house up and burned it down, we built this house back up, a bit at a time. Do we look like we're rich?"

Berry does not look like he's rich. With a yard full of junk cars, an old yellow school bus in the back, the front steps to his house not yet finished (Hoosiers all go to the kitchen door anyhow, unless they are salespeople or other strangers), Berry looks like your typical welder and tow truck operator, your typical self-employed mechanic whose homes are on the outskirts of every backwater hamlet across America.

"You tell me how you make money at this. Here's how it goes. If you was interested in getting into the Klan, you got my number. OK? You call me, say my address is blah blah blah and I'd like some information. So I go into my office, or my wife does it, and we get some literature. Literature costs money. Paper costs money. Then we put it in an envelope and put three, four stamps on it. OK? And you send it out. And they send it back. Then we have somebody check 'em out. OK? That costs money. That costs seven dollars per ap. OK? The donation is twenty dollars, per family. Twenty dollars up front, per family. So I have an application now, for a man, his wife, and two of their children. So it costs a family of four twenty bucks to join, but it costs the Klan about $36 for them to join. So I'm in the hole right from the start."

Backing up a bit, I ask Berry to clarify the application procedure. Just how do you "check out" a potential Klansman? And why bother? We're not talking about the Boy Scouts here, I observe.

"We do have police officers, we do have judges, we do have firemen. We have all walks of life in the Klan," said Berry. With this type of network they can tell what's going on in their communities, he asserts convincingly, as I found out to my own chilling surprise the day after I published my first anti-Klan newspaper article and heard the voice of the Indiana Grand Dragon on the phone, saying, "Why did you print all those lies about us?"

Just how did the top leadership of the Klan get my newspaper article practically before the ink was even dry? It's not like they are on my mailing list. "We have people everywhere," was their reply.

"We want to know who these guys are, because the feds think the Klan is up to no good, and truthfully, a lot of them are," continued Berry. "Believe me. They want that news media, they want to kill people, they want to destroy people, they want to violate other peoples' rights. That's why we are the American Knights. We don't want those people."

Berry, who has been the target of plenty of violence and vandalism himself, maintains he's not interested in having as members people who would abuse a person or destroy his property just because of the color of his skin.

"A man does not know what he is talking about until he has gone through what I have. This house has been shot up. I can show you the bullet holes out in the fence and in the house. It's all on the police record. This house has been burned, all on account of my beliefs."

So just what are the beliefs of the American Knights of the Ku Klux Klan? If not a violence prone group bent on mayhem towards other races and religions, what exactly do they profess to be?

"We are NOT about killing people. We go by the Ten Commandments," claims Berry, who calls himself a reverend, has a card to "prove" it, and opens every rally with public prayer. "We're out there just to get equal rights for our white people. The blacks say they are equal to us. Well, the only way you are going to be equal is compete equally and quit taking and taking from society.

"I feel like, I don't know 'cause I wasn't there, but I feel like I am doing what Martin Luther King done for his people, back in the 60's. Okay? That's exactly **Jeff Berry in action** what we are doing.

"The blacks, and the Jews, and the liberal society is trying to stop us, just like back in them days the whites and the liberal society tried to stop Martin Luther King."

Berry likes to think of himself as a mainstream Klansman, with it being the other Klan groups "out there" that are radical to the point of racial mayhem and violence. He has a whole host of stories of other Klans who go to extremes, he claims, to get publicity. For example, one Klan had its own building along the Pennsylvania turnpike festooned with slogans like "No Niggers Allowed" and "Jewish Parking." After that made a splash in the area newspapers, and the publicity died down, then the local leader went out and burned the place down, crying foul play to the media and blaming the arson on the local black community. "I can't prove it, but everyone knows that's what he did, for the publicity."

He said he's known personally another Klan leader who talks "big and hateful at rallies," shouting out his pat slogan, "any white man who sleeps with a nigger is a nigger," only to rape a black college student later to try to prove what a heavy dude he was to his fellow Klansmen. "Now there is a white man who is a nigger. That's my definition, a dirty, low down person who takes from society."

Berry tells a story about Brad Thompson, his former Indiana Grand Dragon, claiming Thompson used to enjoy telling the media he was a Catholic just to get the extra publicity that the apparent contradiction created (the 1920's Klan in Indiana was an extremely anti-Catholic group). But, Berry claims (and Thompson steadfastly maintains otherwise) he not only was faking his religious background, he also had a drinking problem that eventually destroyed his effectiveness as Grand Dragon. "So when I told him he had to either go into rehab or get out, he couldn't face it, and went around telling the media he had quit, that he had a change of heart, that I was just in it for the money. All that bull was just another publicity thing for him."

But Berry gets a little soft-spoken when talking about Thompson, despite his claim that his former Grand Dragon had done "everything in his power to try to destroy me and my organization." In fact, Berry says he was sorry to see Thompson go.

"It hurt me. He was like a brother to me. I've seen friends die of drugs and alcohol—that's why I'm against that."

Berry says he is against a few other things too. He claims that Morris Dees, head of the Southern Poverty Law Center's *Klanwatch*, has called the American Knights the most dangerous group in the United States. "But that's only because we are the only one's putting on rallies. We are not going out there burning churches and beating up blacks. A person that burns a church to me, is a sicko, 'cause a church is a house of God."

Berry has equal disdain for Nazis.

"These idiots that go around with this Nazi stuff, they are worse than idiots. Okay? Hitler was bisexual. He did a lot more killing in the *Holy*caust than just Jews. He killed his own people. If you didn't fit into what he thought his supreme society should be, he killed

Martin Luther King for white folks?

you. Now that's a scumball, don't you think?"

Berry says the Klansmen of the American Knights are not scumballs. But they know who are. They meet them all the time at the "political rallies" as Klan attorneys like to call their charades on the courthouse steps across America's Heartland.

It's on these courthouse steps where the American Knights find their justification. It's here where the angry taunts of protestors of every color, religion and background feed the frenzy that unites the American Knights of the Ku Klux Klan and propels them to their next Saturday afternoon in the sun, reports Brad Thompson.

"It's an adrenaline thing. It was an us against them thing," Thompson remembers.

The view from the courthouse steps is still a clear one for Thompson. The memory of some two dozen rallies across Indiana, Ohio,

Michigan, North Carolina and Pennsylvania doesn't fade quickly, if ever. The chemistry was real, almost palpable, as the robed Klansmen and women faced the mobs.

"Suddenly we were cemented together, the hate replaces the fear, as it becomes an us against them thing. For every taunt they throw at us, the louder they yell at us, we just become stronger, because it's our rights suddenly they are trying to take away. We are the ones who have permission to be there. They were the ones trying to take our free speech away."

But Thompson isn't quite there yet. After the Angola rally he was merely impressed, not bitten, not yet a true believer.

But he was curious. The rally had whet his appetite, so when Berry closed the Angola rally with an invitation and directions to a barbecue and cross lighting later that evening at his home just a half hour away, Brad convinced Brenda to make the fatal step.

So, like two lambs to the slaughter, off they went to a party at the home of the Imperial Wizard.

Chapter Four:
The Klan that Burns a Cross Together Stays Together

Jeff Berry and armed Nighthawk

I n mid-March of 1998 I intended to travel with Jeff Berry to Cicero, Illinois for a Klan rally that the Chicago area media was warning offered a great potential for violence. Black gangs from the projects had threatened to teach the Klan a lesson. In the course of the ensuing court battle with the city as the Klan struggled to obtain a parade permit, an "anonymous" citizen stepped forth at the final moment offering the American Knights $10,000 to stay home. Berry proclaimed victory and took the money, saying he would use it to print and mail flyers to the community instead of holding a rally.

"Blackmail, that's all it was," asserts Brad Thompson. "Berry just flat-out blackmailed that community."

Blackmail or not, Berry and his followers were still pumped for the rally. Already having planned to congregate from several states as far away as North Carolina to caravan the next day across Indiana to the rally site, they held an impromptu day-long gathering and cross burning at Berry's home instead.

A party at Jeff Berry's modest house is little different from any other Midwestern Saturday afternoon get-together for family and friends, except there is no beer in the house and the children aren't allowed to eat in front of the television set.

Oh, there is one other distinct difference.

When you drive up, a camouflage clad man with a rifle—an assault rifle— steps out from among the parked cars. "You say your name is what, sir? Okay, if you'll just wait by your car, sir, I'll be right back."

This is, after all, the home of the Imperial Wizard of the American Knights of the Ku Klux Klan.

Cameras in hand and a large yellow note pad under my arm, I crack the steamy kitchen door and announce with a nervous chuckle, "Don't say anything you don't want in the newspaper because the press is here."

This announcement only momentarily diminishes the din in the kitchen, and soon I'm being hustled over to the stove and commanded to help myself to a large styrofoam bowl of homemade chili.

"Did you make it?" I ask Berry, as he stirs the pungent mixture in the crock pot.

"Nope. It's Kokomo's finest. Brought over to us by friends," he replies.

He is in charge, however, of the two turkeys bubbling quietly in the stove-top slow cooker, and later that evening when he breaks out his homemade green beans which have simmered on a low burner all day, everyone wants to know the recipe. "Family secret," he grins, blue eyes twinkling.

"Hey—you want a pop? Mountain Dew or Pepsi," my host asks me. "Name it, I'll go get it, we're keeping them cold on the deck in the cooler."

So here I am, with some two dozen Klansmen and women, mostly in their thirties or late twenties, not counting their kids who are pre-teens, on another cold and windy gray weekend in Indiana.

These Klansmen, from Wisconsin, Michigan, Illinois, Indiana and North Carolina, are gathered at Jeff and Edna Berry's house today for a family gathering and cross "lighting," to be followed by a "naturalization" ceremony late tonight (to which I am *not* invited).

Cross-burning, Newville, Indiana, March 1998

There had been a different agenda for today, that got canceled at the last moment. This group was to have been in Cicero, Illinois, for a rally in front of the town hall to protest "police corruption" (their words, not mine) in that grimy working class Chicago suburb. But eight days of court appearances there—with Berry making the drive in his aging grey Blazer, marked by the Klan symbol and Confederate Flag discretely displayed on the rear window, 180

miles across northern Indiana and back again each day—resulted in a dramatic about face.

Although Berry and his ACLU lawyers won the court battle, this roughly hewn but shrewd fortyfive year old Ku Klux Klanner could see he was losing the public relations battle. "I could see someone was going to get hurt, and since I wasn't planning on

Klan mother and daughters preparing for cross-burning

having that be us, I didn't see any sense in getting their town tore up."

Newspaper accounts the week before the rally date had reported gang threats from inner city Chicagoans, who promised to stop the rally themselves.

"We're there to help the town, not hurt it," claimed Berry, who did manage to wring out of the city fathers an anonymous donation from a local citizen to pay up to $10,000 for the printing and private distribution of Klan literature throughout Cicero if the Klan agreed to back off. (Eight months later, the Cicero town attorney, Paul Karkula, told me the literature never got distributed. "Never saw or heard from them again," he said. But Berry did get his money, the attorney confirmed.)

Despite the long drive to the rendezvous point in Newville for many of the Klansmen, only to find out there was no rally, the joviality in the Berry home that afternoon was high. The kids were doing their normal kid stuff, spilling food and tormenting the dog. The adults mingled with pop and chips in hand, with the women admiring Edna Berry's new Presto bread slicer, which she had just purchased to complement her bread making machine, while the men sat around the kitchen table buying and selling Klan and White Power sew-on patches for their leather vests and black pseudo-military attire.

New people constantly walked through the back door, usually without knocking, as the afternoon wore on. Some clutched suit bags for their robes, which they would don for the cross burning when it got dark, and a few carted weapons, a motley collection of automatic shot guns and mail order assault rifles. "You know where they go—keep them in the back room, I don't want to see them out here," Berry said more than once.

In addition to playing traffic cop for the throng of humanity spewing through his house, Berry is not above giving his guests a few lectures on hair etiquette. "You let that hair grow back, you hear me," Berry gently admonishes one young man who sheepishly rubs his hand over his black bristle. "We ain't skinheads—that's for those stupid Nazis."

And for his Wisconsin Grand Dragon, a young man with flowing black locks below his shoulders, Berry laughs, "How much do you think your mamma would pay me if I made you cut your hair?"

So, a jovial atmosphere, no beer, plenty of good, homemade food, and a constant buzz of numerous conversations throughout the kitchen and adjoining family room. In that most of the conversations I tune into are "political" in nature, this could almost be one of those Republican Lincoln Day feeds that Hoosiers hold dear to their hearts.

Only when I join in and ask specific questions does the N word come up, and the whole day I heard no talk at all about Jews or other minority religions until the crossburning speeches, except for the one North Carolina Klansman who assured me it's the "Jewish liberal media" that is out to get the Klan. Explaining that I wasn't Jewish and that of the dozens and dozens of newspaper editors and owners I know across Indiana, the percent of Jews among them is only what you would expect it to be, didn't seem to faze my new friend.

The common thread to the numerous conversations I joined is not any kind of overt hatred to blacks and other minorities. It is more a strong sense of unfairness, a caustic feeling that somehow a whole host of special interest groups have colluded with the government to defraud these people of their basic rights, at least in their minds.

They are eager to tell their stories.

"Do you mind if I tape this?" I ask, "No, no, go right ahead", says Robert Moore, who identifies himself as an itinerant preacher from North Carolina. With full beard, heavily tattooed forearms sporting marijuana leaves, and a black vest littered with Klan patches and pins, Moore speaks with southern dignity belying his backwoods look. "It's in the Bible, sir. God told Noah to take two of every kind and put them on the ark. He didn't say to mix them. God meant for us to be separate."

Hardly able to contain myself I interrupt, "You're not just posturing. You really seem to believe that."

Responds Moore, who holds the North Carolina Klan rank of Exalted Cyclops and is known for his vitriolic tirades at Asheville area rallies, "Yes I do sir, yes I do."

And for Tony Berry, Jeff's son who is anything but today's MTV-addicted, disaffected, sullen teenager, it's the American way to make public statements as the American Knights like to do on the courthouse steps of the Midwest. "When Brad (Thompson) and me went up to the courthouse in Auburn to put that cross there at Christmas, the more they told us we couldn't do it, the more we was determined to get it done."

Get it done they did, to state-wide publicity, when the DeKalb county commissioners under ACLU pressure agreed to let all groups use the courthouse lawns for public Christmas displays.

"The Constitution is a very powerful tool. That's what our forefathers did for us. But the average person now just wants to sit on their butt," fretted the younger Berry. "People just want to watch TV and not do anything to protect their rights. The way I see it, we're just making the county commissioners and such earn their pay, by using the Constitution. We make them think, we make them have to understand the Constitution," Berry feels.

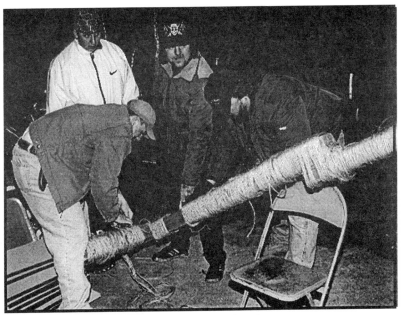

Wrapping a cross with twine

"It's like if we don't use the Constitution, we're going to lose it," he says with great conviction.

A unique way the American Knights like to "use" the Constitution is what Tony's sister, Tonya Berry, refers to as "night riding"— a Klan custom the American Knights revived to considerable Associated Press coverage in 1998. Klansmen in their black paramilitary fatigues invade communities in the dark of night, stuffing their hateful flyers under windshield wipers or into newspaper tubes. According to the AP (Tonya only smiled when I brought the subject up), night-riders have raised the wrath of newspaper publishers in western Pennsylvania and as far away as California who were on the brunt end of angry phonecalls from readers complaining their paper was delivered wrapped inside Klan flyers with the Berrys' phone number on it.

"We've got people everywhere," Tonya's dad reasserted with a grin when I asked him how he did it.

As the evening wore on, and the slow cooker was popped open to reveal succulent turkey for "help yourself" turkey sandwiches with Miracle Whip and Bonnie Bread, a sense of anticipation arose throughout the house. "There's a tightening of the stomach," felt one thirtyish man, dressed in black paramilitary garb with silver Captain's bars on his collar. Every few minutes someone would poke

Armed Nighthawk

his head through the kitchen door to report on the status of the preparations for the cross burning.

No small amount of effort goes into such a task. About four people are required to wrap a person-sized cross with baling twine, and numerous others are put to work wrapping torches.

It's a cold day, and the garage in which these Klansmen and

women are working is not heated. Although they are missing the warmth and the food inside, they don't complain. In fact, they amuse themselves with a steady stream of jokes. "What do you call a black abortion clinic?" asks a woman who is instructing the others on how to wrap the cross. "Crime-Stoppers!" she shouts out to the great glee of the black-clad men and women who are trying to get their meticulous work done by sundown. I point out that their jokes are little different than attorney jokes or journalist jokes, which provokes an unnerving stare from the armed man in fatigues sitting watchfully by the door.

Burlap bags are used in the South for cross burnings, and some places old carpet is used, but twine is considered the best. "It makes the most beautiful lighting, because the flames spiral up the cross," explained Berry.

Back at the kitchen table, amidst the chips and pretzels and pop cans, Berry and his friends are espousing their justification for the Klan, going back again and again to that deep feeling of unfairness that pervades all the conversations in the house that day.

"They can have their Black Miss American Pageant, and no one raises an eyebrow. But if we put on an all-white pageant, you can imagine the howling," said one Klansman.

"Look what's happening at the Auburn Foundry. Everyone there has got to go through some multi-cultural class, because the NAACP made them. Now what's that? What's multi-culturism or whatever? Never heard of it before. That's not right. People aren't going to the Foundry to go to school, they are going there to go to work," pitches in Berry.

"It just gets sickening. Every time you turn around, there's some black who doesn't get his way, and all these organizations come out and support him. But how many organizations is out there for the whites? There's only one, and you're looking at 'em," he adds.

A black-clad Klansman with flowing black hair and dark round wire-rim sunglasses, who hails from California and now works in Wisconsin, where he is Berry's Grand Dragon for that state, worries that the Constitution seems, in his mind, to be interpreted differently for different people.

"There's a double standard that really gets me mad. It's frustrating, it's frustrating," says the young Klaner, who is the proud father of three toddlers. "It is our constitutional right to stand up there on the courthouse steps and say how we feel, yet they want to get out there and say we shouldn't be there, that we don't have that right. But that just means they're delegating to themselves the authority as to who gets to use the Constitution and who doesn't, you know. That just brings us all just one more step towards disassembling the Constitution," he says.

"Damn, boy," interjects Berry. "Does your mamma know you're a genius with all them big words? You're supposed to be a dumb, beer-drinking, truck-driving, trailer trash, expelled biker," he exclaims, to great jocularity among the group. "Don't be using big words like that. You'll ruin the reputation of the Klan!"

In addition to the equal rights issue which they enjoy so much chewing on, there's also a deep sense of economic unfairness driving Berry and his American Knights.

"Like I say, you know, blacks have a right to live where they want to, to work where they want to. So does the whites. But the whites is fighting to get a job, because the government is paying 'em to hire so many blacks, so many Hispanics," is how he sees it. "They're paying these housing units off too. They're getting $2,500 a family to move 'em in there. That's what the government is doing to these towns. The government is the one's blackmailing these towns, not the Klan," Berry adds, looking around and momentarily quietening the din of the other conversations around the house with a throaty roar, "Ain't no one gonna try my green beans?"

But back to the business at hand.

"It don't matter if they is qualified for the jobs or not. All they gotta be is black. Hire a man due to his qualifications instead of the color of his skin," chimes in an automotive technician from the next town up the road. Later this night this same man will be wearing the black robe of the Klan's security force, known as the Nighthawks. He will also be toting a loaded assault weapon, as the occasional car races by in the darkness honking its horn at the otherworldly sight of flames flickering up and down a cross and reflecting on the ghostly white robes of the some thirty assembled men, women and children.

The cross burning —the Klan calls it a "lighting," citing Biblical references to the New Testament where Jesus says, "I am the Light of the World"—is almost anti-climatic, compared to the camaraderie of the chili feed and turkey roast that preceded the night's main event.

In the darkness with only the few street lights scattered around

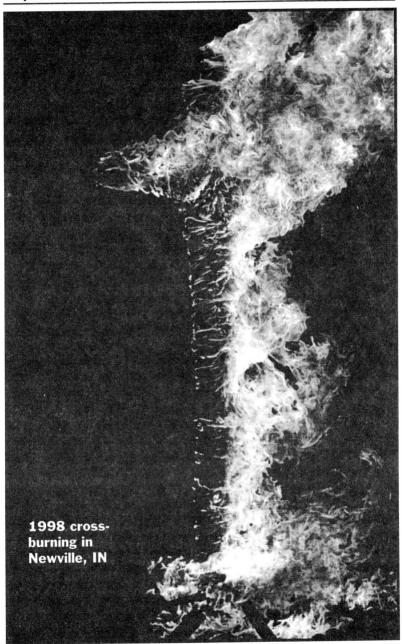

1998 cross-burning in Newville, IN

Newville providing illumination, the robed Klansmen, each clutching an unlit kerosene-soaked torch, march into a circle around the dark cross. Berry issues a few orders to get the spacing right and to intermingle the unrobed guests among the robed ceremonialists.

Berry gives a short speech claiming it is God's will that the races remain pure. Then the Wisconsin Grand Dragon puts in his two cents worth.

"Jesus Christ died for you, right on this cross standing here," he announces. "And who killed Christ?" he asks, cueing himself for a short takeoff on the Jews, a subject which along with homosexuality is also a dear topic to the Klan.

"White Power, White Power, White Power!" concludes his monologue on the ailments of modern society, as thirty voices echo with his.

After a short pause to soak in the blackness of the scene, the Grand Dragon lifts his voice again. "It's a dark, dark world. Out of the darkness comes the light. Each one of you should be proud to be white."

This is the cue at which the Imperial Wizard lights the first torch and passes the flame to the Grand Dragon, who passes it to the nearest robed Klansmen, saying, "This is the light of Jesus Christ. Do you keep this light to yourself, or do you pass it to a brother?"

When all the torches are lighted, the robed Klansmen approach the dim cross and throw their flames at its base.

For an instant there is a breathless pause, the scent of kerosene lying heavily in the air. Then suddenly the flames twirl madly up the cross in a whoosh that bursts into a brilliant ball of fire at the crosspiece.

Reverently some Klansmen kneel at their fiery shrine while others stand sentinel, palms thrust high in the air in their White Power salute of which they are so fond.

As the flames die down, some of the Klansmen get out their pocket cameras to take a few quick snaps of each other and of the still-flickering cross.

"It's beautiful, isn't it?" exclaims one hooded figure, as the others nod silently in agreement, oblivious to the burned, oily stench that lingers unpleasantly on the night breeze.

Chapter Five:
The Making (and unmaking) of a Grand Dragon

Ken Brown (left), director of the Peace Studies program at nearby Manchester College, tries to understand Klan logic, as explained by Jeff Berry (center) and Brad Thompson (right) after a lunch-time interview in Auburn, Indiana, shortly after Thompson took the title of Indiana Grand Dragon

After the Angola rally and the party with its cross burning that same night, Brad Thompson's life was forever changed. Comfortable in his doublewide in a sprawling trailer park on the outskirts of Auburn (the antique car capital of the world with its famed Dusenberg-Cord museum), with his potted plants filling all the windows and his fish tank gurgling merrily away, with Bing Crosby on the tape deck, a lawn to mow and flowers to weed, he didn't know his life was missing anything.

He didn't know his life needed changing.

Sure, he was angry , but he didn't really have anyone to hate.

The few blacks in this Bible belt backwater of Indiana kept mostly to themselves. He had a secure job at a thriving foundry where he felt proud of his work. The modern steel mill under construction nearby was not likely to attract the sort of unskilled, immigrant labor that is often the root of redneck rage.

In fact, in 1995 Thompson's life was a good one, by most standards. His family tragedy was hard to get over, but he still had one small son to adore as well as two teenaged children who deserved his attention.

All in all, there was little to forewarn him that his name was about to become a nationally recognized synonym for racial bigotry.

Oh sure, I told my share of black jokes in high school, we all did. But it was easy to be a closet bigot, you know, when there was no blacks or no other minorities around for miles.

He lived in the West Edge Trailer Park by choice. He'd always lived in a trailer since leaving his parents' home in northwestern Ohio to attend a vocational engineering college, getting married pretty quickly while in school, acquiring an "instant" family and holding down a full-time job over the nearly two decades since then.

An avid reader, his book shelves are filled with an eclectic array of titles like the 50th anniversary *Casablanca* videos, *Homer: The Odyssey, Metallurgy Theory and Practice, The Encyclopedia of Celtic Wisdom, Vegetarian Times, The History of DeKalb County, Asian Health Secrets, Selected Writings of Sigmund Freud, An Anthology of American Presidents, The Jefferson Bible,* and *Stranger in a Strange Land.*

But about the time his son died—Bart was three at the time and Brad was thirty-six—darker titles started appearing on the bookshelves: *Hitler Victorious, Mein Kampf, Hitler's Enforcers, Himmler's Black Order.*

"That's when he quit planting them flowers he loved so," said his wife Brenda.

We was arguing all the time. I was feeling really hateful. So one day, just to get out of the house, I said to Brenda let's go to that Klan rally we had heard about. We couldn't decide if that was a good idea or not. But I had begun reading up on the Klan in Indiana, on the old Klan, and I was fascinated by all the rituals, all that secret order stuff, and I just wanted to see what it looked like firsthand, to satisfy myself if this really was the Klan.

It did indeed look like the Klan.

Angola, a smaller community than Auburn, just up the interstate before the Michigan line, was like many other rural county seats across Indiana. A courthouse not quite an architectural triumph of years gone by, surrounded by sparkling green lawn and ancient oak trees, a modern jail just around the corner. A weekly newspaper office next door, a towering Civil War Memorial in the middle of the circular intersection. Two banks, your obligatory abstract and title office, an ancient movie theater, a podiatrist and a tanning salon across the street. A sleepy atmosphere good for growing corn but not for growing restless on most Saturdays.

But that autumn day it looked and felt like a "beehive" as the Thompsons drove in.

We parked as far away as we could—I didn't want no one messing with our vehicle. So we was late. Everyone was already yelling and it was hard to understand what was going on. But as I walked up I could see the police had everything neatly cordoned off, with that orange snowfence or whatever it is. You had to go through like a chute, and you had to tell the police which side you wanted to be on—with the protestors or with them who was supporting the Klan. I was worried. I didn't know what to do, but since I didn't feel I was really against the Klan, I went in on their side, even though I didn't like being filmed by the television cameras.

That decision so casually made, Brad was hooked. The Angola rally went far beyond his wildest imagination.

What I was hearing totally amazed me; Jeff—Jeff Berry, the Imperial Wizard— was talking. I figured I was going to hear nigger this, nigger that. You know, Jew this, Jew that, down with the Jews.

I figured that's what I was going to hear.

But here's this guy talking more militia, gun rights. Talking about freedom of speech. Talking this Constitutional stuff, which I kinda liked.

So I'm amazed at what I'm hearing. These guys actually sound intelligent. Like they know what they're talking about.

I'd expected to hear a bunch of trailer trash, your typical eighth grade dropout, tobacco chewing hillbilly, with no teeth. But there was several people who actually made sense.

Over-government, too much government, too much taxes. That stuff really surprised me. It really amazed me.

It amazed Thompson enough that when near the end of the rally the Imperial Wizard invited the Klan sympathizers to his home in nearby Newville, a hamlet right on the Ohio border, for a barbecue and cross "lighting," Thompson convinced his wife they should check it out.

I felt right at home. Jeff was a really nice guy, could make you feel real welcome. Brenda and me, and maybe three or four others from the crowd back in Angola, joined up right that night. Here I was, suddenly making a bunch of new friends. It was a real family feeling, and I liked that.

Cementing the bond that night was the cross burning, right in Berry's front yard with the neighbors yelling and shouting insults at them from across the street and several television satellite trucks from Ft. Wayne adding to the carnival atmosphere.

So here's maybe fifteen robed Klansmen, lighting this cross. I start getting goosebumps. I'm in awe, and frightened at the same time. What if my parents see me on TV? What if my work sees me?

But suddenly I don't care, 'cause as the flames climb up the cross, I felt like I was going back in time. I felt like I was a part of history. To me it was a good feeling, a chilly feeling, but a good feeling. It was spooky. That's the word. It is spooky to see robed Klansmen putting a torch to a cross. I can still remember clearly how it struck me to see a woman standing out there lit up by the flames of the cross, in her white billowing robe with her hood off and a gun strapped to her waist. I said yeah, these are my kind of people.

But late that night, driving the 11 miles home west along potholed Route 8 to Auburn, his wife said to him, "Brad, are you sure you know what you are getting into?" Brenda, although she impulsively joined the night of Berry's barbecue and cross burning of her own free will, turned out to know Brad better than he did himself.

When we filled out our applications that night, I really had to pause over what to write down. I had to ask myself just why did I want to join the Klan. Of course I put down things I thought my new friends wanted to hear. You know, to secure a white future for my children and their children's children. To preserve the heritage of the white race, stuff about white power. 'Course I'm trying to impress these guys. Yet at same time, I'm going, duh, just why do I want to join the Klan?

Although he didn't fully understand it at the time, the real reason for his impulsive joining of a movement he really knew only a little about, was that he had a strong but unformulated inkling he was going to enjoy the sense of power, purpose and direction the Klan would give him. Of course, he didn't understand his subliminal reasoning until too late, until the womanizing and drinking and self doubt that followed his election to Grand Dragon drove him out of the Klan twenty tumultuous months later.

The months immediately following his resignation—or his ouster as his ex-best friend, Jeff Berry, Imperial Wizard of the American Knights of the Ku Klux Klan, claims with great believability (whichever, it makes little difference to this tale)—were dark and long ones, filled with doubt, uncertainty and a certain measure of fear.

He couldn't sleep—despite an exhausting foundry job which kept him at work 12 hours a day, six days a week. Once slim and self-confident, easily able to stare down police and reporters with his long hair and freakishly tattooed arms, he gained weight, even to the point of practically being bloated. Some days he was clearly disoriented, either from drink or just pure and simple uncertainty.

It was the uncertainty that he feared the most.

It was like something had jumped into me. And then that something jumped back out. I didn't know who I was, what I was doing any more. I remember the day I was elected Indiana Grand Dragon. I was so happy driving home, whooping and hollering, shooting my gun out the window. I walked back into the trailer and told Brenda that I was really somebody now. In fact I felt like, no, I was convinced, I was D.C. Stephenson (Indiana's millionaire Grand Dragon from the 1920's) himself, come back to life. I had all of Indiana in the palms of my hands. I could SEE it. I was the most powerful man in the state, at least in my own mind. That felt pretty good.

Thompson still relishes to some degree the shadowy images, the pain, the fear, the thrill and the exultation of his initiation into the Klan.

Called a "naturalization," the traditional event took place at the wooded

Klansmen preparing for a naturalization ceremony

home of a longtime Klansman, an unemployed trucker living on disability, from rural Culver, towards the western side of the state.

It was a lot like hazing. Mostly high school stuff. Nothing real violent, but I spent a lot of time blindfolded, being run around in a field, told to sit on a rock and howl at the moon, stuff like that. I still remember how proud I felt when Jeff said of me, "We got a real howler here." At one point they put Stubbs—he's a big man—right in front of me and told me to take off. I didn't know he was there, of course, and I ran into him so hard it knocked all the breath right out of me. And I remember having to pee most of the night, 'cause I'd had four or five beers, but they wouldn't let me do that and the pain was bad. They blew cigarette smoke in our faces, which I didn't like, and another fellow wanted a cigarette so bad he was having the shakes, but of course they wouldn't let him have one.

After several hours of this type of pranksterism, the Klan got down to serious business. Finally unblindfolded, Thompson is taken to a small cabin in the woods—almost like a sanctuary, he said—where he can tell there are three or four armed men standing guard outside. Inside there is an altar, a cross, a barrel and a noose.

Now this is cool, I think. This is where the action is. This is the final test.

Thompson is commanded to get on the barrel. A hooded and robed figure puts the noose around his neck. The rope goes over a rafter. The other end is held by a Klansman—a slightly tipsy Klansman, as it turns out.

Now comes the last act. Answer the next ten questions with the right amount of vigor, then step off the barrel when commanded, with the noose still taut, to show your faith in the Invisible Empire. Now you've earned the right to wear a white robe.

I'm thinking that if I don't pee down my leg, if the guy holding my rope don't fall asleep and accidentally hang me, I can do this.

Here are the ten questions:
• Is the motive prompting your ambition to be a Klansman serious and unselfish?
• Are you a native born or naturalized white, Christian American citizen?
• Are you absolutely opposed to and free of any allegiance of any nature to any cause, government, people, sect or ruler that is foreign to the United States of America?
• Do you believe in the tenets of the Christian faith?
• Do you esteem the United States of America and its institutions above any other government, civil, political or ecclesiastical, in the whole world?
• Will you, without mental reservation, take a solemn oath to defend, preserve, and enforce same?
• Do you believe in Klanishness and will you faithfully practice same towards Klansmen?
• Do you believe in and will you faithfully strive for the eternal

maintenance of white supremacy?
  • Will you faithfully obey our Constitution and laws and conform willingly to all usages, requirements and regulations?
  • Can you always be depended on?

There's an eleventh question: Imperial Wizard Jeff Berry shouts out, "Do you put your faith in the Invisible Empire? If so, step off the barrel!"

I was so anxious to get this thing over with, I had to pee so bad, and I was excited too, that I practically leaped off the barrel, catching the guy holding my rope off guard and nearly strangling myself. That's when Jeff really got pissed off about the drinking and everything.

Thus began Thompson's runaway roller coaster ride. Or more accurately, his Olympic ski jump: Icarus making a spectacular, soaring rush towards the sun with the Klan's fiery cross streaming behind in the wind, followed with little warning by an equally spectacular collision with the ground when his wings melted as guilt replaced his delusions of omniscient power.

I gave freely, pure hate to thousands of people, for over two years, and I got that hate returned to me tenfold. All that hate, all those rallies, made me feel empty, so I had to have more, hoping each time I'd be filled up. Of course, it's just like with friendship, if you don't give anything, then you don't get anything in return, so you end up just bitter and drained.

But that life-changing realization was late in coming, not until he had crisscrossed Indiana, Ohio, Michigan, North Carolina and Pennsylvania in his white robe with the green stripes on the sleeves, his face, revealed behind dark round sunglasses, faintly tinted by the green lining of his open cape. Rushing onward, frenetically careening along his road to power. Eager for the next clash on the courthouse steps, while all the time a little knot clutched at his stomach and a dark cloud lurked at the edge of his awareness: the thought that something wasn't quite right and there might be a price to pay.

Every rally, before we got out there in the sun and under the angry taunts of the crowd, I had to push this little voice out of my head that kept saying, "Now Brad, you know this ain't right." But pretty quickly the butterflies take over, my mind can't think of anything but how nervous I was. Would this be the time someone shoots at us? Can I really put up with all this hate? But just when I couldn't stand it no more the crowd begins to roar, the music is blaring, and suddenly it's like I'm on a rock and roll tour. Nothing but adrenaline pumping.

But back in a troublesome corner of his mind, even as he is eyeing the angry crowd and pumping himself up to shout out the Klan's message of vitriolic hate, he can still hear the voice of his wife Brenda asking that night after their first cross burning, "Brad, are you sure you know what you are getting into?"

Little did he know that he had entered the whirlwind.

A whirlwind that propelled him to the courthouse steps of nearly two dozen county seats across the Midwest in the following 20 months, where he made headlines with his outlandish demands of towns and cities for massive police protection.

It was easy. All I had to do was stop at the local newspaper, show my Klan membership card, and tell them I was in town to set up a rally. By the time they got their wits about them, I was out the door, with the reporters and photographers following me to the mayor's office or police chief's office, where I demanded a parade or rally permit. That always made big news, followed of course by even bigger coverage on rally day.

We always got what we demanded. Plenty of police protection and plenty of news coverage. Everyone was always so afraid of being sued, either by us or by someone hurt in a brawl, which of course was what we wanted. Like when Edna got hit by that rock in Ann Arbor, Jeff could hardly wait to slap a law suit on them.

But there was a price to pay. Thompson, already a fairly heavy social drinker, discovered that vodka could keep him going day and night, which was what it took to orchestrate back-to-back rallies over great distances while holding down a 60 hour a week job.

The alcohol addiction, combined with a growing doubt that he was doing the right thing, finally sent him crashing at the giant

Pittsburgh rally, where the American Knights joined Rob White's Pennsylvania Klan and where Jeff Berry maintains Thompson came completely unglued and useless to the White Power movement.

"He didn't quit the Klan, I threw him out," Berry asserts a year later. "He likes to claim that he saw God at that Pittsburgh rally. The only thing he saw there was the bottom of a bottle."

Thompson no longer denies the drinking—AA has helped him both with the alcohol and the denial—but he claims he did see the light at Pittsburgh. It may have been God, it may have just been his conscience, or it may have been recognition finally that the Klan is little more than a frustrated white man's wet dream. In any event, Thompson's last rally was April 5, 1997.

Armed Nighthawk patrols perimeter of private cross burning

With conflicting emotions of remorse, shame and relief, Thompson rode Berry's bright yellow school bus back to Indiana in tears for most of the ten hour drive, never to don his robe again.

Chapter Six:
Redemption and Deliverance

Eager spectators at Butler, Pennsylvania, March 1998

n the end, no matter whose story you believe or whether you take pieces from here and pieces from there, Brad Thompson had been to the mountaintop.

After all, if you are a Klansman, being Grand Dragon is about as good as it can get. Unless you are a complete egomaniac and can't live without the blue and golden trappings of the Imperial Wizard, wearing the Grand Dragon's dark green stripes on your white robe with your cape lined in even darker green is a lot like sitting on the right side of the throne.

It feels mighty fine.

The view from the mountaintop, from any perspective, is a good one. It is an appealing sight. An almost Biblical scene spreads out below the courthouse steps: the phalanxes of police parting the waters in front, the shrieking mob behind.

And Thompson at first was pleased with what he saw.

Moses must have felt like this. Jesus we know was tempted. When he was at the brink and the Devil said jump, he gave it some thought, I'm sure. I know I felt one hundred feet tall. There was times I felt I could just reach out and scoop up everybody in the palm of my hand. Police, protestors, the whole town, the whole state. We were invincible.

Indeed they were invincible.

The crowds roared when the Klan told them to. The police marched when the Klan struck up their martial music. And the press wore out their motordrives when the Imperial Wizard, clad in shimmering blue, and his wife in gold, unfurled their blazing Confederate and American flags in the snapping breezes of a sunny Saturday afternoon.

Their lust for power—for respect—was an insatiable craving.

Nothing else could drive mere mortal men and women from town to town across the Midwest at such a frenetic pace. Nothing else could drive out the fear of facing yet another unruly mob, never knowing for sure if the helmeted police hiding behind the glare of their Plexiglass face masks hated you more than the angry young protestors with their vile language, earrings and weird tattoos. Nothing else could make up for the sick, sweet roiling in your stomach when you first looked out at the crowd and wondered if this was the day the metal detectors had failed to find the one gun aimed at you.

Power, respect, adulation. These were more important than safety, love and family.

And it was clear that the colorful trappings of the Imperial Wizard were the pinnacle of what Thompson thought then was the power and the glory.

I just worked my butt off for Jeff. I spent thousands and thousands of dollars of my own money, making phone calls, buying stamps, buying gas, on his behalf. He was that kind of guy—he made you want him to like you.

But toppling Jeff Berry from his self-proclaimed throne was a risk Thompson never even dreamed of taking, not even in his wildest moments of self-aggrandizement.

You just can't believe the grief you get when you lead an organization like this. There were times I just don't see how Jeff stood it. Our own people would just go crazy at us. There were times me and Jeff just couldn't do nothing right, even the piddliest of things, like deciding where the next rally would be.

But if you know your Klan history, this wasn't nothing new. A lot of Klans that you'd have thought really had their act together over the years, just suddenly up and disappeared when they'd start fighting among themselves. Organizations like this you get people that just don't want to do nothing but tear each other down.

There was enough of that going on that I didn't need to invite any more.

Thompson still remembers the backlash he got after he suggested making some changes in the rally format.

We was reviewing the tapes after the first Ft. Wayne rally, it was early in 1996, and I noticed some of the guys were smoking while waiting to make their speeches. That just looked disgusting. It made us look just like what people already thought we were. Nothing but white trash. So I suggested we not smoke in public. I thought we should look sharp. Like respectable people.

Thompson—always a superior strategist who felt the medium was equally as important as the message—was stunned by the ridicule that followed his suggestion.

You'd a thought I'd suggested we paint our faces black or something. So here I am, Grand Dragon. The top dog in Indiana. And I can't make a simple little request like that, to clean up our act a bit, without coming off as some sort of lunatic.

Or like when I wanted us to stop cussing at the rallies. People didn't come to hear us cuss. Some I knew were offended, and I was *afraid they wouldn't hear our message if they were offended by all our bad language and everything. So I tried to levy a fine of $5 a cuss word. I wanted us to clean up our act and try to act like a respectable group, so that if we really believed in our message people would listen to us. But it seemed to me we didn't really care. 'Course it didn't help none that Jeff was our biggest cusser.*

Although not willing to put up with the type of power struggles that are endemic to the Klan and other radical fringe organizations—power struggles that historically have kept these groups splintered and which, fortunately enough, reduce their effectiveness—Thompson still could have kept strutting his stuff on the courthouse steps across the Midwest if he had put his mind to it. But that was the rub. He didn't care to put his mind to it anymore.

In the almost three years I was in the Klan, it drained me financially and it drained me emotionally. I'd become a totally different person. You seen the pictures of me, with my family, Brenda and the kids, before I was in the Klan. I even look different now, and I don't like that none. I been out a year, and I still don't feel fully recovered. I still have trouble sleeping.

Thompson admits that with the advantage of hindsight it's easy to see why he got out of the Klan, even at the pinnacle of his power. But he also admits he enjoyed the power and missed it to the point of distraction at first.

I was a smug Grand Dragon. There was nothing I couldn't do. I liked nothing more than dealing with some big-shot police chief or mayor. I'd walk in like I owned the place, and pretty soon I found out that the more brazen I was the more they'd treat us like royalty. It felt like they was just eating out of our hands, 'cause they knew and we knew, that if they didn't give us everything we wanted, all we had to do was make a few phonecalls to the media and the ACLU to complain about our Constitutional rights being violated and our free speech being shut down, then there'd be even bigger turmoil. I liked that feeling, that I was just as powerful, if not more powerful, than they were.

'Course now I have the guilt of hoping I didn't bring nobody

down on account of my own arrogance and lust for power.

Thompson to this day thinks it is that element of power, symbolized by a Klan rally, that is the Klan's biggest draw.

You've got to think, there'd only be fifteen or twenty of us up there on the courthouse steps, yet there might be as many as 300 police out there guarding us. I think people thought that if we could

Police break up fight at Butler, PA

command that much response from the authorities, then maybe we really could do something for them. 'Course what the people didn't know was that we was just there to get more members, to get more money.

There wasn't nothing we could really do for them.

Mark Mitchell, a 22-year veteran sergeant with the Indiana State Police tasked with coordinating security for Klan rallies, agrees with Thompson that the Saturday afternoon spectacles are a charade. "It's their right, but all they are doing is coming to these towns, with their misguided comments, to hold membership drives."

Thompson's first inkling that the whole rally thing was considerably less than met the eye came while he was driving to the June, 1996, Ann Arbor rally where Edna Berry's head was split open by a rock.

I'll never forget Jeff Berry saying to me as we drove up, 'Wouldn't it be nice if we could just get these towns to pay us to stay away?' I was stunned. That's extortion, I told him. I didn't want to go to jail, but worse than that, just the fact he made the comment really bothered me. I really thought we was doing something important. Protecting people's rights and all that. But suddenly it just looks like we're in it for the money. I think that was the first seed.

Then of course Jeff sued Ann Arbor for eight million dollars, all over a little bitty cut to his wife's head. But I never did see how the police or no one else could have prevented someone from throwing a rock at us. I mean, what could we expect? We were trying to provoke these people. That was the whole point.

The seeds came slowly at first, as little things. Little things that started eating on him. Such as Berry's offhanded comment about being paid to stay away—which was exactly what Cicero, Illinois, did two years later, to the tune of $10,000. Or the cavalier way he used his wife's injury to try to line his own pockets. Little things that caused Thompson to wonder if somehow he wasn't missing something.

Slowly but surely the luster of being Grand Dragon was fading.

It's like anything else, you can get sick of it, particularly doing it all the time. It got to where we was driving back and forth to Pennsylvania, back and forth to North Carolina and South Carolina and never seeing nothing. I wanted to stop and do the Civil War battlefields, things like that. After all, we was supposed to be the Klan, you know?

But we never had no time. It's like we had to be on the move every second, be some place on time, to meet with the police, meet with the mayor, meet some new recruits, or something like that, and there was never no time for just us. We'd leave after work Friday, drive all night to Pennsylvania or somewhere, talk with the police in the morning, do the rally in the afternoon, do a cross lighting that night and then jump in the cars and head right back home.

It got to where I couldn't see the use of any of it anymore. One rally looked like another. We never had the time, not even the interest somehow, to be real people.

Thompson never missed a day of work from the Auburn Foundry, working as many as six 12-hour shifts a week. He proudly displays his certificates of achievement to prove it. But he clearly didn't have the energy reserves (except when his engine was fueled with vodka) of a Jeff Berry, who was a band leader growing up with his aunt and uncle in Garret, Indiana, and was accustomed to a road life before he took up the Klan full time. And of course it didn't hurt Berry's energy level any that as Imperial Wizard he was able to keep most of the money that was coming in from the talk shows (Appendix One), memberships, and sales of the Kloran (Appendix Four) and robes.

Jeff likes to claim there's no money in this, but that's just not true. He might not live the high life. But he's got a nicer house than most of his members. He's got his lake cottage. And he doesn't do much else but do the Klan full-time, although his wife has a good job.

The dollars must roll in.

After the May 11, 1996 Portage, Indiana rally where the Klan got lucky and tapped into racial hysteria when an eight year old white girl was raped and killed by a black fugitive from Chicago shortly after the rally date was announced, 140 strangers accepted the invitation to drive seventy miles that night to Culver, Indiana for a cross burning and membership sign-up.

Say Jeff got $20 each from those new members. That's $2,800 in one night. And I know that Barry Black, who was with us representing Pennsylvania's Keystone Knights, sold $1,000 worth of Klan regalia. Yet you couldn't believe some of the people we were taking in that night. Some had their guns with them, and most were talking nigger this and nigger that. My wife Brenda said that if that's all they could think about, then they needed to just get right back in their cars and drive back to Portage.

But Jeff, if it was the color of green, then anything was okay with him.

But at a deeper level, it was more than the fatigue, the frustration, and the dawning realization that some of the motives of the Klan's top leadership weren't entirely pure, that was bothering Thompson. It was the thought that there had to be a price to pay. He was right.

At New Castle, in 1996 on a bright sunny June Saturday afternoon, the Klan caught hell. They tried to stage two rallies in one day, and when they were late for the second, they got into a shouting match with the police, who wanted to search them again for weapons. Rather than cooperating, Berry marched them off around the town with some supporters in tow, and no one was prepared when a band of protestors jumped them.

It was crazy. We knew the crowd was angry. Because we had been way late setting up. But we didn't know they was laying for us. The police broke up some pretty good fights, Jeff got arrested for fighting, and we were all pretty shook up afterwards. But none of that slowed Jeff none, and although I urged us to mend our ways and do things on time and cooperate with the police, nothing changed.

On some of those long drives across the Midwest, which often started before dawn if the rallies were in southern Indiana or several states away, Thompson had time to reflect upon the quality of the company he was keeping.

Although he got along well enough with Berry at the time and still tries to stay on his good side out of respect for old friendships, it always bothered him that Berry's checkered past included a stint as a paid police informant. Berry is well known among law enforcement agents in northeastern Indiana for the number of drug and theft cases he helped make following his own arrest on theft and stolen property charges in 1989.

People were always telling me—guys I already knew and guys I met in other Klans— that I didn't want nothing to do with Jeff 'cause he was an informant, a narc. I didn't let that bother me none, but I thought about it. I know someone has to do it, but it kind of made me wonder if he was really trustworthy or not.

Another leader in the American Knights worth thinking about

Police make an arrest in Butler, PA

according to Thompson is Robert Moore, the Exalted Cyclops from North Carolina. Moore, according to the Southern Poverty Law Center's *Klanwatch*, publicly threatened a crowd in Asheville he would "wipe out in eighty-eight seconds" those protestors if they showed up again at one of his rallies. "And God forbid if there's any children there," he added.

Now he's an interesting person. He claims he was in North Carolina's White Knights and quit them because three of their members got convicted of burning a church, and maybe he did. But that threat he made at Asheville, that means the Klan will never have another rally there. Free speech is a thin line, and he crossed it. You can't incite people to riot, and since he did that, they just have to show up and rile the crowd just one time before they get arrested. You've got to wonder what he was thinking.

Moore, who quietly eschews any thoughts of violence when he explains his views one on one ("I'm just an itinerant preacher") nonetheless comes from the North Carolina tradition of Klan violence. It was in Moore's own lifetime, 1979 to be exact, that Klansmen from the Tar Heel state fired on a group of protestors in Greensboro— not far from Moore's own hometown—killing five.

Indiana State trooper Mitchell confirmed Thompson's comment that free speech only goes so far. "It's one thing to state your opinions. You're free to do that. But when you start urging other people to commit violence or say that you're planning on it yourself, well, we've had to warn Mr. Berry about that a few times."

Thompson admits that his wife kept urging him to open his eyes and look more carefully at these people he called his best friends.

You know, you're around these kind of people all the time. Some don't have jobs and aren't planning on getting one. Some are smoking pot, some are doing worse than that. There's guns everywhere, and you just don't know what these people are thinking.

At first you think it's cool. We're all one big, happy family. But after awhile, everyone turned out to be trying to get something.

A lot of people were real jealous of me, thought it was way cool to be the Grand Dragon. Or jealous of Jeff or mad at him for something or mad at me 'cause I was close to Jeff.

It wasn't always just flags blowing in the wind and us standing there on the courthouse steps in our neat robes and the press taking pictures and everything. Sometimes it was just a mess. A whole lot of aggravation.

And everyone has guns. I had guns. Brenda had a gun. We all had guns in our cars. If someone wasn't going to use a gun on us, then it was just a matter of time before we used them on each other.

Getting closer to the root cause of his disquiet with the Klan, Thompson confesses some days he was downright afraid.

I always wondered, particularly standing up there on the courthouse steps, when someone would get angry enough to take a shot at us. After all, that's what we were there for, to make people angry. So after that time we was driving away after the rally in Peru (Indiana) and a carload of blacks and Mexicans chased us waving shotguns out the window, I started giving it even more thought.

Then there was the rally in Pittsburgh, April 5, 1997, which was the final straw for Thompson. That was the rally where the Klan's own hate was returned in a tidal wave ten times larger than the American Knights had ever experienced. That was the rally where Thompson, already filled with self doubt, realized he had come to the brink and didn't like what he saw when he peered over the edge.

This was a big surprise. We wasn't in Indiana no more . We saw that the minute we got off the bus. There was 12,000 people out there— ten times as many as we done seen at any rally before. Half of them black and all of them angry. You couldn't believe the roar of all that hate. They was screaming 'white trash go home', 'fuck the Klan', 'KKK sucks', all at the same time. The roar was so horrific, that you could imagine if the gates of Hell opened right now, that would be all the misery and all the hate you would hear coming out.

Jeff was just as high as a kite on all that uproar and hate, strutting around saying, 'Can you believe this?' But I told him right there I for one thought we had gotten more than we had bargained for.

Although the Klan that day escaped Pittsburgh without incident—the police kept the protestors so far at bay you could hardly make them out individually, he recalls— it was Thompson's last rally.

Already desperately trying to reconnect with his spiritual roots, he became completely unnerved when he read in the *Pittsburgh Post-Gazette* that the Catholic church there had said a special mass for the Klansmen.

That was it for me. If they could pray for us, after the Klan had been historically anti-Catholic, if they could ask God to forgive us for what the Klan was doing to their community, to their people, then I knew that God was intentionally peeling me apart like an onion.

Thompson wasn't just afraid of his so-called friends and their guns. He wasn't just afraid of the protestors and their angry out-pourings of hate. He was afraid God was pointing a finger at him.

I had spent nearly three years giving freely of hate to thousands and thousands of people. Thousands of people that I didn't even know. Now I heard God telling me it was my turn.

And there was one other small problem. Brad Thompson had run out of hate. He simply never had enough hate to maintain a Klan identity under the weight of his own personal fears and his frustrations with his fellow Klan members.

One year before he got out of the Klan, when he was still at the height of his power as Grand Dragon, I met with Thompson and Berry both at a Bob Evans restaurant in Auburn, Indiana, where the waitress was so frightened by the sight of these two rough look-ing, tattooed men well known as local Klan leaders that she never did get our orders straight. Berry was pleasant, even offering not to smoke at our table, although I had repeatedly referred to him in an earlier article as "The Imperial Whooping Crane." And Thompson asserted that he had never had a racial incident of any kind. (Al-though how he would describe a Klan rally, then, escaped me.)

"I've never in my life had trouble with another person because of their skin color. I work at a foundry. I work alongside blacks, Iranians, Hispanics. I never think about it. It's not a big deal," Th-ompson said over a vegetarian lunch, completely mystifying me. Like if this guy isn't thinking about it, then why is he spending every minute of his free time organizing these outlandish rallies across the country? I didn't get the logic.

After the Pittsburgh rally, none of it was a big deal for Thomp-son anymore. He was a broken man.

Jeff Berry claims Thompson was a drunken man.

He'd like to think that. It's true—I was a basketcase, and I did drink. But that's not what got me out of the Klan. I was tore up, because I knew what I had done was just flat wrong. That little voice said louder and louder to me at every rally, 'Now Brad, you know this ain't right.'

Jeff likes to claim you can't quit the Klan, that the only way you can get out is to be thrown out. He likes to say he threw me out because I wasn't Klan material. I don't think anyone is really Klan material when you think of it, because the Klan just isn't what it says it is. It's all about petty jealousies and greed. It's all about feeling important at someone else's expense.

When I realized the Klan is none of those things the Klan and their attorneys like to say it is, that selling trinkets is more important to them than free speech, then I got out. It doesn't take no really heavy thinker to see the hypocrisy. When you are in, and if your eyes are open, then you see it, believe me.

Once Thompson decided to quit he sent everyone on his mailing list a notice that he had left the Klan over differing opinions of what issues the American Knights should be stressing. And he went on a new whirlwind tour of his own.

Cross lighting ceremony

This time his efforts were spent alerting the media that their towns were being duped by the Klan and their opportunistic attorneys into thinking they had to roll over and play dead.

Don't believe these attorneys when they tell you they defend the Klan out of concern for free speech or whatever. That's a lot of bull, and everyone knows it. They get paid. Sometimes Jeff had to pay them, sometimes they billed the city, sometimes their organizations, like the ACLU, paid them. But they always got paid. Don't lose any sleep over the Klan's attorneys. It's just another element of the whole greed thing that drives the Klan.

Once he was out, Thompson had three tips for the media, things he wanted the press to tell their communities.

Dave Peyton, columnist for the *Herald-Dispatch* of Huntington, West Virginia where the American Knights planned a rally just a few months after Thompson took off his robe for good, summarized Thompson's tips this way:

• The reaction the Klan hopes for at any rally is an angry protest. "It energizes them," Thompson told the columnist. "It gets them wound up so they can continue speaking. If they're left alone and nobody protests, they'll talk about 15 minutes and run out of things to say."

Preparing for a cross lighting

• The best reaction from a community is a "unity rally"—a festival celebrating diversity, often sponsored by a community's ministerial association, at a location across town from the Klan rally. "These rallies are successful in that they show how the community feels about the Klan. They definitely bring the community together," Thompson told Peyton. (During the vitriolic Butler rally, described in Chapter Two, the unity rally across town that day attracted a number of participants nearly equal to what the Klan drew, Pennsylvania Sate Police told me later.)

• It's worth the effort to try to deny the Klan a permit. "The Klan is hurting financially. There's a good chance they won't have the money to hire lawyers to take the case to court."

These kinds of comments to the press earned the wrath of the Klan.

C. Edward Foster, Pennsylvania Grand Dragon of the Keystone Knights of the Ku Klux Klan, told the *Pittsburgh Post Gazette*, "You

Klan family lights cross

won't believe the hate I can put out on someone." Foster—who knew Thompson from the Portage, Indiana rally that attracted one hundred and forty new members—proudly proclaimed to Post writer Dennis Roddy that he was the author of a flyer circulated in Thompson's hometown accusing him of quitting the Klan in order to form a chapter of a gay-rights organization.

That hurt me, I nearly got evicted from my trailer. And there was more. My car was covered with graffiti night after night, and one night when I was at work someone came to my door and told my wife we would all be killed soon. It wasn't exactly fun getting out, but the alternative weren't no picnic neither.

I'd laid in bed, night after night, wide awake consumed in grief, trying to figure out what possessed me to allow the Klan to capture the heart of my very soul. I still don't know the answer to that.

What I do know is that I cost communities in Indiana alone some $600,000 in overtime pay and extra equipment for police protection (the Indianapolis Star puts the figure higher than that, throwing in $185,000 the State Police have incurred in extra expenses but never billed to the communities they helped protect). *Just think what that money could have been spent for, instead.*

And I still don't understand why I supported an organization, with all of my effort for almost three years, that has committed so many crimes against humanity. I'll never be able to explain that. I know I'm nearly wore out trying.

What I hope, no, what I pray for, is that my experiences, telling about them, will save some poor soul from the trouble of going through the same things I've went through.

Believe me, when you pour out hate, you get it back ten fold. And if you're anywhere near a normal person, then you are left feeling nothing but empty and drained. It's not a good feeling. It's not worth it.

Being in the Klan is like watching a fire in an old dry field. You burn fast, tall and hot. And when the fire passes, nothing is left inside you but gray, dusty ashes.

Chapter Seven:
The Light at the End of the Tunnel

Anti-Klan statement in Butler, PA

T he light at the end of the tunnel isn't very bright, but it does flicker with a certain consistency.

Although there are not many like Brad Thompson out there publicly repenting of their deeds and exposing the Klan, there are a growing number of communities which have put up a united front against hate mongering.

LaGrange, Indiana, was the first community to just say no to the

American Knights.

A burly ex-marine who has pastored the Missionary Church there for the last nine years had a brain storm one Wednesday evening as he met with his worship committee several weeks before the Klan's 1996 appearance in this pastoral county seat set in the midst of Indiana's Amish country.

"We were talking about how frustrated we were, that the law was on the Klan's side and that we seemed powerless to do anything," remembers Pastor Bradley Ulick. "But we knew that you didn't fight hatred and bigotry by drawing a line and shouting back obscenities."

Ulick felt there just had to be a better way. "How about a community picnic? " he suggested to the group. "Some place nice, away from the Klan rally, right at the same time they're downtown."

And from that simple suggestion a new movement was born.

So threatened was the Klan by Ulick's suggestion to hold a Unity Picnic—the picnic idea got more pre-coverage in the local press than did the upcoming Klan rally—that Ulick received several phone calls from the Klan leadership, complete with Biblical overtures and false flattery, begging him to speak at their rally.

"I told them I didn't need to stick my head in a sewer to know what one smells like," he responded.

When that ploy didn't work, the Klan alternately threatened him and tried to swear out an arrest warrant against him after they spread the rumor he was setting up a countermarch to break up their rally. He got phonecalls from people who identified themselves as the Imperial Wizard and also as the Grand Dragon.

"That's the Klan for you. They call you up and expect you to wet your pants when they tell you who they are, and when you don't, then they don't know what to do," Ulick, who learned his street smarts in the rubble of Beirut, remarked. "These people are just bullies. Sure, there are some, not many, who are perfectly capable of carrying out their threat, but that catches up with them when the courts strip their organizations and the leadership of everything they have," he added.

So the LaGrange Missionary Church went ahead with their planning, getting the Lions' Club involved and inviting the community to an old-fashioned hot dog roast, with entertainment for both the kids and the adults, ranging from Indian games, square dancing, clowns, and balloon sculpture to a Civil War reenactment.

Was it a success?

"The press—what little of it came to our picnic, most wanted to see confrontation at the Klan rally—asked me that same question," responded Ulick.

"So I challenged them to look with their own eyes. Did they see anyone angry? Did they see anyone violent? No—what they saw was some 2,000 souls of all denominations and colors loving each other and having a happy, peaceful time."

Ulick said the Lions' Club estimated there were between 1,600 and 2,100 people at the Unity Picnic (not bad for a small town of 2,200 residents), judging from the number of flyers they handed out that morning to the participants, compared to the 300 or so people the press estimated were at the Klan rally.

"That really made the Klan mad as hornets," said Ulick.

Something else made the Klan mad that day too.

The newspaper there gave them no ink. None before the rally. None after the rally.

"I learned a long time ago not to let people make a whore of me," said Publisher Bill Connelly, who has been poking his pen into the inkwell at the *LaGrange Standard* for forty years.

"This is what the Klan wants you to do. They expect to come into your town and get you to make a big deal of it, to facilitate their message in the rest of the media. I just wouldn't play," Connelly reported.

"Why would I want to pull their freight wagon?" he asked.

"They can have their free speech if they want it. They are free to buy an ad in my newspaper," he added.

Connelly, who is a hands-on publisher and knows nearly everyone in this small county-seat that was the home of Indiana's earliest Jewish community, said he heard absolutely no negative comments from his readers about his approach to Klan coverage. "Sure, I think the sheriff would have appreciated a picture showing what a good job his boys did keeping the peace, but everyone generally seemed grateful I didn't put the Klan's trash in the paper."

Although the *LaGrange Standard's* approach to Klan coverage was somewhat unorthodox, the idea that surfaced in LaGrange to hold Unity Picnics to counter Klan rallies has spread to the point that it has become the standard response. In fact, the Southern Poverty Law Center, which tracks hate groups with its *KlanWatch* report (see Internet Appendix) lists Unity Picnics as among the most important ten steps a community can take when faced by threats from the Klan.

In Butler, Pennsylvania, where Jeff Berry took his American Knights on a bright sunny spring day twenty-three months after I was first introduced to these misguided misanthropes in LaGrange, the Klan was greeted by a full page ad in the local newspaper. In big bold type on page 3, the ad urged residents to attend a "Celebration of UNITY" in the local park at the same time the hooded hatemongers were shouting on the courthouse steps. Signed by the pastors of some 80 area churches, the ad read like this:

"Hatred and division are evils that must be removed from every aspect of our community life. As spiritual leaders, we must speak without reservation or evasion against any effort that promotes hatred or intolerance in any form, especially when it is done in the name of God. When hatred is proclaimed by those who call themselves Christian, it insults all Christians and threatens all people.

"All our faith traditions call people to love one another in the name of God. We recognize that all men and women are created in the image and likeness of God and call upon all people of faith to unite in opposition to hatred and division.

"We choose to unmask all forces that would divide and separate. We reject all groups that proclaim superiority by reason of race, religion or national origin to any other group of people. We call for all people to work and pray for racial justice and unity so that the human dignity of each person is affirmed.

"We pledge, each in our own way, to expose the evil of racism for what it is so that society is changed through the transformation of individual hearts and minds. We are all brothers and sisters."

Did it work?

You be the judge: the Klan—many of whom had driven ten hours the night before from Indiana—spoke to a sparse crowd that the Associated Press pegged at 600 protestors and supporters. That's barely one half of one percent of Butler's population. Most residents obviously had better things to do that day.

Other Midwestern communities are trying an even more proactive approach, not waiting for the Klan to come to town or for the possibility of a second round.

Four Indiana communities have gotten themselves into a tussle with the ACLU by passing anti-mask and hood ordinances. Goshen, Elkhart, Logansport and South Bend resurrected the old ordinances after spending huge dollars on overtime pay for police protection during Klan rallies. Jeff Berry predictably responded, according to the Associated Press, that his rights were being violated. "Everybody in this United States has a right to engage in political speech anonymously, unknown, or whatever," he told the AP.

Although such ordinances have been upheld by courts in Louisiana and Georgia in recent years, according to Mark Potok of the Southern Poverty Law Center, in practicality they do little more than illustrate a community's response to the Klan.

"The fact is that most Klansmen around the country are willing to march or rally with their hoods raised, so it has not been an entirely pressing issue," said Potok to the national wire service.

My personal experience with Klansmen and women, both at rallies and at private events, is that they are quite open about their beliefs, being strongly convinced that their views are correct. They rightfully note that the same laws which protect blacks, Jews and others from discrimination also protect them. Thus it is quite common to see many unmasked and unhooded Klansmen at American Knights' rallies.

Such attempts at regulation, of course, play right into the Imperial Wizard's hands. Berry loves to point out that there is nothing illegal about belonging to the Klan and that opposition groups are all too eager, in his mind, to take away the rights of the Klan while "screaming" about protection for black rights and gay rights.

"Why can you have an all-black Miss America contest, yet if we was to put on an all-white beauty contest, we get called racist?" Berry has asked me on more than one occasion, to illustrate his point that Klan followers are unfairly stigmatized. "How come it's okay to be a Black Panther and not okay to belong to the Klan?" he loves to ask.

One Midwestern community that is looking at a multi-fronted approach towards encouraging unity is North Manchester, Indiana, home of Manchester College, site of the nation's oldest Peace Studies Institute.

Host to Martin Luther King's last public appearance in Indiana before his shooting death in Memphis, Tennessee a month later, Manchester College was hit in the spring of 1998 by a hateful e-mail message which appeared in the electronic mailboxes of some

107 minority and international students. The perpetrator, who was never sought when the county prosecutor decided—without investigation—that no crime had been committed, wrote:

> *Your time is up. The niggers, the spics, and the fucking immigrants are through. You have caused enough trouble in this town and your fucking days are numbered.*
> *White fucking Power!*
> *Die Coons Die!*

The e-mail came the morning after a weekend of bar fights that many claimed were racially motivated, although no arrests were made in these incidents either. The Klan was NOT implicated in these incidents, although a young factory worker was seen on the ensuing (and hysterical) television coverage waving a Confederate flag at the edge of the campus.

Not withstanding the somewhat murky origins of the incidents, however, the town council and the Chamber of Commerce, prompted by local religious, joined forces with college staff, students and administration to create a community response.

Part of the response was the collection of 1,400 typeset signatures (from a town with 6,000 population including the 1,000 students at the college) for ads placed in six area newspapers, including *Frost Illustrated*, an ethnic publication based in Ft. Wayne, condemning bigotry and racial hatred.

The ads read like this:

> *"We condemn the message of hatred and racism that has challenged our college and community in recent days. We cannot responsibly remain silent and so we offer these clear commitments:*
> *• We are committed to a college that will fulfill its stated mission of developing an international consciousness, a respect for ethnic and cultural pluralism, and an appreciation of the infinite worth of every person;*
> *• We are committed to a community that shares these values and will welcome, encourage and support all who live, study, and work in our town;*
> *• We are committed to a college and a community that come together to dispel misunderstanding, confront hatred, and advance the best ideals of a truly democratic society."*

The public response of the town's thought leaders to the brawls and hateful e-mail was swift and sure. An ad hoc coalition was pulled together by college dean Stan Escott to address the issues. He said the purpose of the group, soon to be known as Manchester Together, was to "counteract divisiveness" and to develop both short term and long range plans "to rid the community of the root causes of hate and bigotry."

"This kind of thing diminishes us all," stated Judie Silvers, executive director of the town's Chamber of Commerce. "We need to constantly educate the community about diversity issues and make new people here feel they are a valuable part of our community," added Don Rinearson, president of the North Manchester Town Council.

The group successfully called on the resources of the local chapters of the Fellowship of Reconciliation and Education for Conflict Resolution to begin the process. It began meeting twice-monthly on a regular basis.

However, the coalition lost its way momentarily when an avalanche of regional and national press coverage alarmed the community, prompting some to talk about "Salem witch hunts."

A proposal floated to establish a Human Rights Commission for the town, to monitor housing and other types of discrimination, caught particular flack, with business leaders fearing it would be too powerful and legalistic. Some church groups assumed it was a front for a gay rights movement in town. Even the college's top administration privately labeled the proposal a "dumb idea" for a town the size and nature of North Manchester.

With the group then mired down in debating the merits of action versus education, Jeff Hawkins, the pastor of the Zion Lutheran Church, pointed out the positive aspects of the dilemma (as pastors are wont to do): "Conversation is a good thing—it needs to happen."

So, on that note, my own two-year odyssey on the trail of the Ku Klux Klan ends where it began—back in North Manchester. The words of the Lutheran pastor in his red brick church across the street from my office ring with renewed clarity.

These are issues worth talking about.

Conversation by its very nature is an educational experience.

I don't think it will convert many Klansmen—that's not the point. But listening to the pain and frustration of marginalized people, including Klan sympathizers, is part of an important process. Acknowledging other people's pain is a healing experience. It's this kind of healing that can reach those who aren't yet True Believers—those who are in the middle between the extremes of these issues.

And a little levity doesn't hurt.

Lew Borman, executive director of the Ft. Wayne Jewish Federation, used laughter to break the Klan's spell when Brad Thompson, still wearing his robes of white and green, wrote the Federation to issue a threat and to blackmail the northeastern Indiana Jewish community. He said the Klan would sue if the Federation didn't donate some of its Lemonade Fund money raised during a counter-event to an American Knights rally in Ft. Wayne.

Borman shot back, "The proverbial bottom line is this. We are an organization that has a seventy-five year history in this area of working on issues and values of social concerns. We will not be intimidated by hate groups in any way."

When Thompson called to offer a compromise, asking for a share of the money collected by the Federation at the Klan rally to be donated to a charity in the Klan's name, Borman was struck speechless by the outrageous silliness of the proposal.

"Lew Borman just outright laughed at me. That took my power away," Thompson admitted later.

Taking the Klan's power away has been what this book is about.

After two years of talking to Klansmen, police, public officials and victims of the Klan, my own belief is that the Southern Poverty Law Center has come up with the best approach to neutralizing Klan activity.

Here is their ten step program, reprinted with the Center's permission:

1. STAY AWAY FROM WHITE SUPREMACIST EVENTS

When hate groups announce plans to march or rally, people are often unsure about the proper response.

It is tempting, but counterproductive and often dangerous, to confront white supremacists at their public events.

The principal reason is that violence by counterprotestors is becoming commonplace at white supremacist rallies and marches.

Some anti-racist demonstrators travel from rally to rally, actually hoping to provoke violent confrontations with the racists.

Others may attend the event simply to protest peacefully, only to find themselves enraged by the inflammatory rhetoric and caught up in the violence.

White supremacists are skilled at turning such situations to their advantage, gloating that the violence came from protestors, not the hate group.

In Denver, violence marred the 1992 Martin Luther King holiday when angry protestors at a Klan rally attacked each other, bystanders and police.

One anti-Klan demonstrator was seriously injured by another counterprotestor, and three police officers were hurt.

Twenty-one people were arrested.

Order was restored only after police used nightsticks, tear gas and Mace.

At a neo-Nazi rally in Auburn, New York, in September 1993, enraged protestors in a crowd of about 2,000 attacked the racists and pelted police with rocks.

The crowd also chased the white supremacists' cars and threw bricks and bottles.

Two counterdemonstrators were arrested.

Two Auburn residents, one a Jewish man, rescued a female neo-Nazi after she was struck in the face and kicked.

Some of the counterdemonstrators threatened to kill another man who helped the woman.

Finally, it is important to remember that the media often cannot distinguish between curiosity seekers and the hate group's sympathizers when estimating the crowd at white supremacist rallies.

Peaceful protestors can easily be mistaken for hate group supporters.

All this can be avoided by simply staying away.

Then the event, attended only by white supremacists, will lose much of its appeal to the media.

2. ORGANIZE AN ALTERNATIVE EVENT

To discourage attendance at racist events, communities should organize a multicultural gathering that encourages family participation.

Ideally, it should be staged in a different part of the city, at or near the time of the hate group's rally or march.

Examples of such events include the following: • In Columbus, Ohio, citizens created a Unity Day in response to an October 1993 visit by the Knights of the Ku Klux Klan.

Hundreds of people participated in activities that reflected the city's diversity.

The program featured rap music, traditional Hebrew songs, a school's Spanish choir, the city's opera and a gay men's chorus.

The city used grant money to fund most of the event.

• In Pulaski, Tennessee, the birthplace of the Ku Klux Klan and the site of numerous Klan rallies, residents have countered these events by emphasizing the community's unity and its disgust for the Klan.

On the day of the Klan rally, downtown merchants have closed their businesses and staged a brotherhood march that is now an annual event.

• In Colorado, a ski resort offered discounts on lift tickets and rentals as incentives to keep people away from a 1992 Klan rally.

Some communities plan ecumenical services where people can express a united front against hate.

Such services should incorporate all of the town's religions.

• In Wallingford, Connecticut, townspeople held ecumenical services in December 1993 in response to a series of hate crimes.

• And in Texas, a woman invited thirty-five churches to a prayer vigil on the same night as a Klan cross-lighting ceremony.

"I figured prayer was what these people needed, and a whole bunch of it would be better," she said.

3. DON'T TRY TO STOP WHITE SUPREMACIST EVENTS

People often try to keep white supremacists out of their area by pressuring city officials to deny parade or rally permits.

This tactic is seldom effective.

White supremacist groups have won scores of lawsuits on First Amendment grounds against communities that attempted to block their public events.

Ultimately, the event will be held anyway, and the furor surrounding attempts to stop it will only gain more publicity for the hate group.

4. PLACE ADS IN THE LOCAL NEWSPAPER

When hate crimes occur, citizens should consider buying an advertisement in the local newspaper.

The ad should emphasize unity and support for the crime victim as well as the target group to which the victim belongs.

It should also convey the message that hate crimes will not be tolerated in the community.

Newspaper ads can also counter the publicity that hate groups attract.

These ads should denounce the organization's bigoted views and should run on or before the day of the white supremacist event.

5. FORM COMMUNITY ANTI-RACISM GROUPS   Another way to effectively oppose hate groups and hate crime is to form a citizens' anti-racism group.

The organization should be composed of people from every race, religion, and culture in the community, including gays and lesbians, who are frequent targets of hate crime and hate groups.

The group should stress cooperation and harmony and discourage confrontational tactics.

Some anti-racism groups, formed in response to a particular racial incident, hate crime or hate group, have found ways to sustain their sense of unity and purpose indefinitely.

One such group, the Friendly Supper Club in Montgomery, Alabama, was founded to ease racial tensions after a violent incident involving city police and black residents.

With the goal of improving the city's strained race relations, black and white residents began meeting over dinner at an inexpensive restaurant to discuss issues affecting the city.

There was only one rule—each guest was asked to bring a person of another race to dinner.

The Friendly Supper Club has been active since 1983.

6. RESPOND QUICKLY TO HATE CRIMES WITH A SHOW OF UNITY   Concerned citizens should quickly put aside racial, cultural and religious differences and band together to fight the effects of hate crime on a community.

In some areas, non-Jews have joined their Jewish neighbors to scrub swastikas and graffiti off synagogues.

Elsewhere, white and black residents have gathered at black churches to remove racial slurs and to rebuild black churches burned by racists.

In mostly white Castro Valley, California, residents organized a unity march in September 1993 after a black teacher's car was vandalized with Klan slogans.

In February 1997, in response to a spate of vicious hate activity on the California State University campus at San Marcos, university employees committed to making donations to an anti-racist organization each time such activity occurs.

They made their first donation to the Southern Poverty Law Center.

And in Palm Springs, California, a group of high school students wore ribbons they had made to symbolize unity following a brawl between blacks and Hispanics in October 1993.

"We're trying to show the students who are causing a problem that we're not going to stand by and let that happen," the school's student body president said.

"If enough people come together, we can overcome this."

7. FOCUS ON VICTIM ASSISTANCE

Hate crime victims often feel isolated, so it is important to let them know that their community cares about them.

"Network of Neighbors," a volunteer organization formed in 1992 in Pittsburgh, Pennsylvania, offers emotional support to hate crime victims.

Commander Gwen Elliott, head of the Pittsburgh police department's hate crime unit, said the group offers a much-needed service.

"A lot of times, (hate crime victims) don't know how the court system works.

"They need support and help in dealing with their anger, so they don't go out and do something irrational," Elliott said.

Since hate crimes are not often solved quickly, volunteers should encourage victims to be patient and cooperative with law enforcement officers handling the investigation.

8. RESEARCH HATE CRIME LAWS IN YOUR COMMUNITY AND STATE

Some states and cities have broad hate crime laws that cover a wide range of incidents.

Others have limited statutes that allow only data collection or cover only specific acts of vandalism.

In many states, if a bias crime is prosecuted under a hate

crime statute, additional prison time or stiffer fines can be imposed.

Five states have no hate crime laws.

In those states, a racial slur written on a black family's house is treated as simple vandalism.

If a community does not have a hate crime law or the existing statute is weak, citizens should urge their elected officials to support strong bias crime legislation.

9. ENCOURAGE MULTI-CULTURAL EDUCATION IN LOCAL SCHOOLS

Because more than half of all hate crimes are committed by young people ages fifteen to twenty-four, schools should be encouraged to join the fight against hate.

One way is to offer multicultural materials and courses to young people.

Educators have learned that once differences are explained, fear and bias produced by ignorance are diminished.

Many schools are already teaching students to understand and respect differences in race, religion, sexual orientation, and culture.

The Southern Poverty Law Center's Teaching Tolerance Project provides educators with workable strategies and ready-to-use materials to help promote tolerance and understanding.

10. FIND UNIQUE WAYS TO SHOW OPPOSITION

It is important to remember that there is no single right way to fight hate, nor is there any one list, including the one here, of sure-fire approaches that will work in every community.

The suggested responses in this report should be adapted to local circumstances, and community leaders should always be open to fresh approaches to fighting hate.

With a little imagination, many people have found unique, and often humorous, ways to voice their opposition to bigotry and racism in their communities.

Some recent examples include the following:

• In Connecticut, a community distributed anti-Klan bumper stickers reading, "Our Town is United Against the Klan."

• In Lafayette, Louisiana, the editors of the Times of Acadiana said they "felt terrible" about running an advertisement placed by a local chapter of the Ku Klux Klan.

So they decided to split the proceeds from the $900 Klan ad

between two of the hate group's archenemies — the NAACP and the Southern Poverty Law Center's *Klanwatch* Project.

Bayou Knights Grand Dragon Roger Harris apparently found the approach a little hard to take.

"I have to swallow hard. I really do," Harris said.

• In Springfield, Illinois, a couple gave the Louisiana idea a local twist by turning a January 1994 Klan rally into a fundraising event for three of the Klan's foes — the NAACP, the Anti-Defamation League and the Southern Poverty Law Center.

Based on the adage, "When life gives you a lemon, make lemonade," the event, lightheartedly dubbed Project Lemonade, was modeled after the common walkathon.

The project's donors pledged money for each minute the Klan rally lasted.

The longer the rally, the more money was raised for the three anti-racism groups.

The project's creators, Bill and Lindy Seltzer, said that the response was excellent and that pledges were collected from throughout the state.

Hate crimes and hate group activity touch everyone in a community.

For that reason, people of good will must take a stand to ensure that hatred cannot flourish.

As German Pastor Martin Niemoller said:

>*"First they came for the Communists, but I was not a Communist—so I said nothing.*
>
>*Then they came for the Social Democrats, but I was not a Social Democrat—so I did nothing.*
>
>*Then they came for the trade unionists—but I was not a trade unionist.*
>
>*Then they came for the Jews, but I was not a Jew—so I did little.*
>
>*Then when they came for me, there was no one left who could stand up for me."*

Appendix 1:
The Jerry Springer Show

by Worth H. Weller

$5   Holiday Inn Chicago City Centre $5

JERRY SPRINGER SHOW
*Not redeemable for cash
*To be used in the Centre Cafe, Corner Copia or Room Service
*Does not apply towards purchase of LIQUOR
*gratuity not included

300 EAST OHIO STREET CHICAGO, ILLINOIS 6061

$5   N⁰ 4128 $5

Time Magazine thoroughly trashed the *Jerry Springer Show* in a four-page color spread for its March 30, 1998 issue, shortly after the tawdry spectacle's ratings surpassed the *Oprah Show*. The review was written apparently in perverse recognition that no other syndicated talk show had ever topped Oprah's popularity before. But Brad Thompson knew Jerry Springer's real-time soap opera was pure theatrical trash from the first time he rode the limousine to Chicago in 1996.

"Ah, you just couldn't believe it. You'd have to be there to understand, but it was crap, just pure trash," Thompson recalls, recollecting how set up he felt when he saw the studio layout with its special black seats where the actors and other pre-screened people sat in the audience within easy reach of Springer and his teleprompted questions.

Trash or not, however, when Thompson and his wife Brenda appeared with six other Klan families from Jeff Berry's American Knights, they tapped a cash cow "like you couldn't believe."

Thompson in his role as Grand Dragon helped negotiate with

the Springer producers to get the seven families on the air. He and Berry had to settle a special deal to get the Klan's 219-337-KKKK number flashed on the screen. The number was aired opposite the Southern Poverty Law Center's phone number, not making the Klan very happy.

But it was worth the compromise.

"I don't think it was on more than three to five seconds, but we logged over 6,200 calls requesting Klan literature and membership when the show was broadcast," Thompson convincingly claims. He should know. He and Berry manned the American Knights' high-tech phone system (complete with caller ID) in Newville for two weeks running, often resorting to answering machine tapes to get a rest. "We had so many envelopes to mail out, that the post office in Auburn complained, telling us only businesses could do these types of big mailings. So we had to drive to all the area post offices to divide it up," he remembers.

So just what is the allure of the show?

Time Magazine summed it up in just one word: *fights*. Thompson saw plenty of those and was nearly in some himself.

One of his most vivid memories from the show unfolded in the audience, where the robed Grand Dragon from Wisconsin—who had actually been the point man to get the group on the air, only to find himself shunted off into the audience (without a limo ride)—was already working under a head of steam when a black man seated two rows back started spouting off. "Ole Mike had had enough and he jumped up and grabbed that dude by the throat and was about to throttle him, when the guy startled him by saying 'Hey man, back off. I'm just acting. It's just a job, OK, pal?'," Thompson reports Mike told him after the show.

Thompson said the Springer deal was actually "pretty cool" at first, with a lot of high-powered behind the scenes maneuvering ahead of time to get on the air

Mike McQueeney, the Wisconsin Grand Dragon (who also helped broker the deal 18 months later with Cicero, Illinois, that put $10,000 into the Klan's coffers) helped put the Springer deal together by making the initial contacts and talking up the idea of having Springer confront a group of Klan families, women and children included. Two Springer producers drove down to Culver, Indiana, where they met Berry, Thompson, and several others at the Rodney Stubbs farm—the site of Thompson's "naturalization" into the Klan the previous year. That was in August, of 1996, and the producers returned a few weeks later to film a crossburning and returned again the following month to film a rally at Knox, Indiana, and to cement the deal. "I was surprised how tough these women were. They were young but they stood right up to us Klansmen and made no bones about the fact they were in charge. The only thing we got our way on was the phone number—Jeff said there would be no deal without that—but they got seven of us families to agree to come to Chicago, for no pay."

Actually some money did change hands, and Thompson has the copied checks to show for it.

Each family got paid $100, plus got $85 in cash and a similar amount in "Springer" money to spend at the Holiday Inn near the NBC studios in downtown Chicago. Also, each family got one night's deluxe lodging there, plus a limo ride to and from their homes in Indiana.

"Like fatted lambs to the slaughter," Thompson remarked exactly two years later.

After the glow of the limo ride wore off (a glow helped along by the copious liquor supplied en route and in the hotel room), Thompson began to smell a rat. The special black seats, the instructions from the producers to stare hostilely at the audience and wear angry frowns, the admonitions from the stage manager to the live audience (most of whom had gotten their tickets for the show a year ahead of time and had been lined up that morning already for hours to get a front row seat) to applaud when told and to shout and scream on demand. The hooded and shielded tele-prompter that followed Springer wherever he prowled up and down the aisles, carefully cropped out of the picture that was fed a month later to the TV viewers. "These were clues that the whole thing was a charade, although I was so pumped the first time I didn't fully comprehend right away that it's all staged," Thompson claims.

The following spring, after Brenda's on-air, off-the-cuff remark that she was in the process of adopting Brad's youngest son prompted a storm of angry mail from Springer viewers resulted in a return engagement, Thompson was sober enough to pay more attention to the details.

Springer, when introducing Brenda for the return engagement as a Ku Klux Klan mother who was adopting an infant (Joey was already three at the time), pumped the audience by suggesting Klan mothers abused their children by brain washing them or worse. "I was enraged," Thompson reports, eyes growing wide at the memory. "Which is what he wanted to me to be. Because when I angrily confronted a producer, they filmed that without me knowing it and sold it on one of their 'Not for TV' videotapes. I had people coming up to me at the Foundry, wanting me to autograph their tapes. It was wild. No, not wild, it was disgusting."

So in the end, the *Jerry Springer Show* and the American Knights of the Ku Klux Klan had something in common: they both were hoaxes, making promises to their audiences—implied or otherwise—that they never intended to keep.

Appendix 2:
Klan Regalia and Officers
By Brad Thompson

Klan leadership in front of the Butler courthouse

List of Colors and Stripes of Klan Robes

My first experience with the robe was back in 1995 at my first American Knights Rally. There was quite a color scheme - almost Halloween-like. Dark blues, and bright purple, and jet black as well as the all-standard off-white. There were also military fatigues.

The history books don't go into great detail about the stripes or the colors other than black and white. I soon found out why. It is the second Era Klan of Col. Simmons that introduced the robe colors and officer stripes. If you were to go to a Klavern Meeting (club house meeting), you would don your robe of basic white. Upon arrival, you would put your officer's robe on, if applicable. Depending on rank of office you would have x-number colored stripes.

After going through the ritual of entering the meeting room or den, all being hooded and robed in their proper attire, you were aware of who the officers were as identified by the stripes on their sleeves. Get it?

But, something happened to the Second Era Klan as this minister turned fraternity organizer with internal power struggles, theft of large sums of dues and internal decay. In the pre-WWII era of FDR's administration, the Klan got caught up in an income tax evasion scandal, amounting to a sum in excess of $600,000 owed Uncle Sam. This was how Al Capone was brought down. Because of this, the Klan's Georgia charter was revoked and all the robes, regalia, symbols and secret rituals that were patented under the 1915 charter could no longer be used.

This meant that in order to keep from getting sued for the outstanding tax liability for the usage of this fraternity stuff in the future, some drastic changes had to take place. An added item here to note: A short time after the 1915 charter was issued, there were two separate other charters issued - one in the state of Louisiana and the other in Florida. To keep from getting sued for patent infringements from the other klans, they had to use ever so slightly different rituals and regalia. Although the Kloran (handbook) stayed pretty much the same, the robes changed drastically. Only one group remains today that defiantly uses not only the 1915 Kloran and regalia as well as the secret rituals, but also the original robes and colors with the same officers' stripes cut from the original patterns of the 1920s. This group is the International Keystone Knights of the Ku Klux Klan Inc., based out of Johnstown, PA and headed by the very strict iron fist of the colorful Rev. Barry E. Black whose great uncle, the honorable Hugo Black, served on the Supreme Court in the 1920s, and was a Klansman as well.

So as to not confuse you any further, there are about 127 active Klan groups in the nation. All these groups have a leader, most of whom are called Imperial Wizards. Most of these leaders use whatever suits their fancy when it comes to robes, colors and officer's stripes. All, however, use the standard white robe. The page that has a listing of robe colors and stripes is what I put into standard at Jeff Berry's request to make it to where the American Knights would stand out from the rest of Klandom.

I also, at Jeff Berry's request, rewrote the Kloran to suit the modern needs of the retail empire of the American Knights. I spent a total of 180 plus hours doing this. I used the 1960s U.K.A. (United Klans of America) Kloran, a 1952 E.L. Edwards Kloran from Georgia, and a William Hugh Morris Kloran. Plus I added some very unorthodox changes at Jeff Berry's request that made a lot of other Klan groups very upset and angry with Jeff Berry.

Klan robe, 1998

What I didn't realize until months after I got out of the Klan was that the American Knights Kloran separated the old from the new. I gave the younger members an easy-to-understand way of setting up a Klavern and making robes. On the other hand, it did cause total hate and resentment from the older members who branded Jeff Berry as a common "thief and patriot for profit" for changing their most sacred Kloran rituals and robes.

The whole of the matter is pretty petty. The 1920s Klan had headlines of sex scandals, stealing of Klan funds and leaders suing each other over money. Now, seventy-two years later, history seems to be repeating itself again.

The following is an overview for the different officer's robes and stripes with color schemes, as well as the most common secret words that are still used; almost all of this can be found at your local library. It is with much hesitation that I share this, because I feel that I helped to create a monster when I simplified the Kloran for the American Knights.

At $35 a crack for this piece of work (the Kloran), I made it simple for Jeff Berry to run his empire. He has a flourishing mail order business and is doing well with sales of memberships off the Internet as far away as California and parts of Europe and Australia. Robes sell from $85 up to well over $100.

I will start with the "secret" stripes and colors of the officer's robes. The national Imperial Wizard Jeff Berry has had three different I.W. robes since I have known him. He has to change, not only the size (bigger), but graduated to some very gaudy color combinations to set himself apart and draw the attention of the people. He uses lavender, or a deep dark blue with very "loud" yellow stripes, five on the sleeves. The woman's national Imperial Wizard's robe is the inverse of the color scheme. Put some eye protection on the next time the American Knights come to rally in your town. Even though the A.K.'s ladies' auxiliary robes are the inverse of the men's, the Knight Hawks robes jet black with red stripes are the same for both sexes.

OK. Now before I go any further, I am going to attempt to explain the different levels of hierarchy or anarchy and the stripes on the sleeves (see insert page). The imperial officers have five stripes on the sleeves and all or some robes have stripes on the bottom hem, denoting either years of service (five years), one stripe or a stripe given by the N.I.W. for a special achievement or ass-kissing.

Example: The Imperial (national) Knight-Hawk (security) = black robe would have five red stripes on the sleeves and red under the cape, just like Super Man's (smile). All robes have capes with corresponding colors under them which match their stripe color. So, the National Imperial Wizard, five gold stripes. The Imperial Knight Hawk, five red stripes and National Exalted Cyclops, black robe with five orange stripes as well as the woman's auxiliary go by this formula for their robes to this day. Keep in mind that the Knight Hawks Woman's are the same as the men's.

Now we go to the state level: the Grand Dragon of the realm or governor of the state; the Grand Knight Hawk Head of state security- four stripes does it.

The county level has three stripes. The Grand Dragon has an assistant - a great Titan (white robe, three black stripes, or a hydra white robe, three green stripes). The E.C. has a white robe with three orange stripes; the E.C.'s assistant has a white robe with two orange stripes. If you look at the attached list I wrote up, you can see that it is very straight forward and set up very simply. Remember that the bottom stripes are for special services, and/or years of service (five years) per. This is reserve for only the American Knights, of course.

Confused yet? Remember all you need to know is that stripes on the sleeves mean you are in the presence of an officer; stripes on the bottom indicate years of service or special services to the order. The black robes are the SS of the group and the white robes with colored stripes are the pencil pushers. Five national, four state, three county and two assistant county and slick sleeve a plain knight. I set up the American Knights to maintain simplicity so as to not confuse the new members and the old.

Officers

Next, I want to explain that the KKK is the most complicated entity in the world today. It is a combination of an imperialistic dictatorship. The National Imperial Wizard is the supreme boss, similar to John Goddy, Al Capone and the Dahli Lama. He can change the rules in the middle of the game in order to win and come out on top. All other Imperial officers and Imperial board members are under his rule, and he is able to overrule state tribunals (courts) etc. What Jeff Berry says, goes. The American Knights belong to him - lock, stock and barrel.

The state officers are like governors, but have actually no authority to think for themselves or make any decisions without prior approval from his lordship, the self-proclaimed "savior" as he likes to be called - Jeff Berry. Most of the state officers' duties and all officers under him are simply to generate dues for the national office. All monies collected - every red cent - goes to the National Imperial Wizard. The rest of the duties of all the lower officers is to spend money out of their own pockets for the benefit of the leader. And push their pencils, as well as risking all to being the front man for the National Imperial Wizard when he feels unsafe about the media attention. The lesser officer sets up the rallies, sets up literature drives, etc.; he does the dirty work for the National Imperial Wizard.

The E.C. does the county work for the Grand Dragon, but he still has to answer to the boss man also. When I was the Grand Dragon, I put a whole lot of faith in the E.C.'s. I always tried to get away from the hierarchy of the pompous National Imperial Wizard. I put my trust and faith in those under me and never once questioned decisions made by them. I always lead my men; I never pushed them. I considered them my backbone.

Example: I can't drive 200 miles to settle a dispute with a sheriff about an upcoming literature drive, so I let the E.C. of that county take care of it. As the old saying goes, "Shit rolls down hill, and the heat rises off of it".

There is a very simple way that I had learned from Jeff for keeping control of one's officers. For the prestige of a single stripe and paying the National Imperial Wizard the price, you can be in the front line, an "in your face Klansman," a leader among the commoners, while all the time national headquarters is raking in the money and the publicity—all at the junior officers' expense.

I will say this. Some folks would say that I am soured because I did not get the publicity and the so-called glory (money) from my stint with the A.K.K.K.K. Well, I say to them that in this group, or any other of the Klan splinter groups of same, you can judge a good officer by the size of his or her "phone bill". It all amounts to the exact opposite of what the late president John

John F. Kennedy stated, "Ask not what your country can do for you, but what you can do for your country". In the inverse, Jeff Berry asks this of his officers, "Ask not what you can do for the Klan, but what you can do for the National Imperial Wizard."

In closing, the order, rank and duties of the officers in some ways are very complex - to the degree that they are fooled by the flim-flam and the pretty colors of the robes. The bottom line is this. The National Imperial Wizard has the final say on all things. It is more like a cult than as what they try to portray. It is not a fraternity, as compared to the Masons or Oddfellows. It might be a religion since Jeff is a "real" bonafide Reverend of the Universal Life Church. He paid his $20 for that. Even Jim Jones was a bonafide Reverend.

The other Klans have their Imperial Wizards too. Each one of them does their own thing. The American Knight Ku Klux Klan (A.K.K.K.K.) is the most feared and militant, headline grabbing Klan group in the country, and what's scary is, some of the other groups are starting to follow Jeff Berry's example!

Appendix 3:
The Klan and the Internet
By Brad Thompson

The American Knights have a major presence on the Internet

I want to explain that I visited more than 300 web sites. Most dealt with white supremacy in some shape or form. Most inter-connected with each other by links. In my investigation of these sites I noticed that certain sites had hundreds of these links that could be traced back to the top 20 most popular visited sites. The top five web sites boast of tens of thousands of worldly visitors each year.

It depends on what you type into the web search engines. KKK, Ku Klux Klan, Klan or white-power. You can even type in anti-Klan. This intrigued me to the point of almost fanaticism. I would spend almost every waking moment sitting in front of my computer searching and printing volumes of this type of information. I did all of this during non-Klan function days or weeks.

The American Knights Web Site
www.americanknights.com

This web site has floated up and down in the top five web sites for more than 1.5 years. This site has gone through some drastic changes in order to compete for the cash flow of white supremacy. It starts out with some spectacular graphics and at the end, before you enter, there is a disclaimer. It does a good job of getting your attention. Most surfers don't go past the first page unless it is eye-catching. Once one gets hooked and goes past the first page, there are several options to choose from: history of the Klan, its political platform, up and coming events; a little taste of old Klan rituals and the meaning of some of the most used and open of the symbols; letters to the web site, good and bad, with their answers from the Imperial Wizard; an antique pamphlet with some selected writings and poetry from Wild Bill Hoff, the Imperial foreign representative for the International Keystone Knights of the KKK.

A statement from I.W. Jeff Berry along with an actual membership application that can be printed out is available. This, along with a money order made out to "cash" will put you on your way to becoming a 90-day probationary member. To fulfill your obligation, you not only must buy a $90 robe from the national office, but also must attend one of Jeff's functions, or create your own. Jeff Berry claims around 15,000 paid applications have been sent to him in less than a year - A very big accomplishment indeed!

Pastor Thom Robb - Knights of the KKK
http://www. kukluxklan.org

Pastor Robb claims to be the real and only true Klan. The pastor is slick; he has several web sites with slightly different names. One example is the Northwest Knights of the KKK. My first exposure to the Klan over three years ago was on his Indiana web site out of Salem. It was one of three at the time on the worldwide web. It boasted of having ties with David Duke and showed an early picture of him standing in front of Big Ben over in London, England. This crude site, at the very end, offered an application and gave an address as to where to send your money. The very last part really got my attention, as it showed more than 40,000 visits in eight months. You can see why it is so competitive for guys like Jeff

Berry and Thom Robb to constantly be on top of the heap. At one time both of their sites were almost identical (generic), but now it is like going to a home and product show.

For the armchair/closet racist, these sites offer membership, Klan merchandise, history, jokes, chat rooms etc. The list of hate sites are many and they are all linked in some way or another. For example, Jeff Berry, who is a self-proclaimed Nazi hater, has links to Nazi web sites. Thom Robb, who is the self-proclaimed only real and true Klansman, has links to other Klan sites as well as links to the Aryan Nations and the WOTAN (Warriors of the Aryan Nations). Both have links to the Skinheads, Christian Identity, Black Separatists and different foundations like NAAWP of America (National Association for the Advancement of White People) which is headed by David Duke. All claim to have some sort of friendship or ties with Duke. Jeff Berry claims to have been naturalized by Duke; other Klan groups scoff at this as a falsehood. But behind the scenes of these top dogs of the Klan, they do talk to one another and brag about their latest adventures into the taxpayers' pockets.

As of Dec. 1997., SPLC. claims there are 474 registered hate groups. I think that this is by far an underestimate. There are groups that use front names, like a group in Rockville, IN that uses a conservation club as a front for the Klan.

The First Amendment is being put to the test on the web. In 1996, a 20-year-old Orange County man named Richard Machado, while a student at the University of California, sent hate e-mail to fifty-nine Asian students. He threatened death and harassment. In his first trial, he was acquitted. Even this year a similar incident took place at Manchester College in North Manchester, IN.

The web has a few alternatives. There are a few anti-Klan web sites and a few very smart surfers who cause disruption and mayhem to the pro-Klan sites. I have visited a few of those web sites and was surprised to see my name and picture in a couple of them. I have always believed that there are two sides to every view point. It intrigued me beyond belief at my first visit to the S.P.L.C.'s site.

Southern Poverty Law Center (SPLC)
http://www.splcenter.com

This site has greatly improved since my first visit well over a year ago. SPLC is also known as the Klanwatch and the Militia Task Force. Communications for different Klan functions, like literature drives and rallies, come to the center from local law enforcement agencies and groups like the NAACP. There is also a packet that is sent to towns that are targeted by the Klan - this is the "Ten Ways to Fight the Hate." I was surprised when I got my copy off of the web. Almost all of the towns where I set up the Klan rallies were very smart indeed. The majority of the Indiana communities already practiced some of these ten ways. I imagine that this list was compiled over a period of time resulting from the close monitoring of Klan rallies, literature drives, and the attacks of other hate groups and the response of the communities in question.

This web site has quite a few sections loaded with information. A section on intelligence reports lists of all hate groups by state and marked on a U.S. map, legal actions taken in the past, teaching tolerance to people, etc. The complete section on the Ten Ways to Fight Hate has examples of uses, and goes into a paragraph or two on how to use each or all.

Example: LaGrange, IN Rally

Not only did the local newspaper use a cartoon to slam the Klan, but in the same cartoon it advertised the unity picnic. LaGrange had a religious unity picnic that brought together the Amish people and all other religious faiths under one banner. I was, and still am, amazed at this, since I actually lived in this area for a couple of years. The Amish folks would always shy away from others and always kept to themselves; this was a positive thing that came about from something so negative.

A.R.A. (anti-racist-activist)
www.angelfire.com/ms/pukerock/index/html

My first experience with this group of college kids from Ohio State University was at our April 20th, 1996 Bryan, OH rally (where I was born). With contacts throughout the whole country at the time, via the Internet, this was my fourth rally and my first time to speak publicly. I always looked out into the crowd to figure out what makes people tick, and maybe learn who to recruit. At this rally (see the cover of this book), my attention was caught by about twenty young men dressed quite smartly in army fatigues. Since I was always pro-militia in my views, I was very impressed. I figured that they were militia since there is a militia group in my home county.

Well, soon it was my turn to speak. I had to be shoved out in front of the mike. While I was giving my vile scared-to-death-little-hate speech, I could hear these guys chanting A.R.A.—A.R.A.—A.R.A. I actually thought that they were saying N.R.A., so I saluted them since this gave me a dose of courage to go on with my speech. I then told them that I believed in N.R.A. 100 percent, or something like that. This in turn confused these boys who had come to protest the Klan. I did not know until later on that day, after I read one of their pamphlets, that these college students had driven two and one-half hours from O.S.U. to

protest the Klan and pass out an alternative message opposite to mine. I was enraged and impressed at the same time, since these guys had already known about our next up and coming rallies before some of our members did. LaGrange, IN and Portage, IN. It was the last time that I ever saw A.R.A. at any of the rallies that I set up.

The only thing that I can say is that they have the right idea. I can see the limits that we put on college students. It was almost too much for me. We rallied too much and too fast and too far in 1996 (they couldn't keep up, and I almost couldn't).

The pamphlet that A.R.A. distributed at the rally in Bryan had a statement about money. "Give us your money; lots of it, so we can fight the racists." I could see why they would need it; it costs money to travel, etc. I know, since I spent a fortune "running with the Klan."

The News-Journal Anti-Klan Home Page
www.communinet.org/News_Journal/klanindex.html

Around the late summer of 1996 I was getting the idea that it might be time for me to buy a computer. One of our more colorful members, David Roach, who was also a minor Ft. Wayne politician, brought me something that surprised me - several computer print-outs taken off the Internet at the Ft. Wayne library. They were from the "Anti-Klan Home Page" maintained by the North Manchester, Indiana, News-Journal. At the top of the first page was a picture of Jeff Berry and me standing outside of the Auburn Bob Evans restaurant. I was very shocked, so then I was bound and determined to buy that computer and printer so that I could see for myself what was out there.

Right away I purchased the necessary equipment needed to start my own office. I then proceeded to figure out how to go about obtaining my own copy of the news coverage of not only the Bob Evans interview but the LaGrange rally that got the News-Journal onto the trail of the Klan. I was really intrigued by the fact that a small town newspaper could not only have its own internet web site, but that it also made claim to being an Anti-Klan web site as well.

I then visited this site often and told all my friends about it (because it had a picture of me) and it was a really neat site. It is not too complicated, real easy to the eyes and has a lot of neat links.

I then began realizing that other newspapers' web-sites might have articles and pictures of the American Knights, so I started surfing the towns we had rallies at and started my Internet scrap book of news articles.

I used the News-Journal's web-site as a resumé when we were dealing with the Jerry Springer Show's female producers.

To surf for Klan articles, both for and against, I use Yahoo as a search engine 90% of the time, but when you type into any of the many other search engines "Anti-Klan," you get the North Manchester News-Journal. There should be more sites like this. I am proud to say that the web master of this page is not only the author of this book, and I his collaborator. I am also proud to call Worth Weller my friend.

Appendix 4:
The Kloran
as revised by Brad Thompson

Jeff Berry (center) and Brad Thompson (right)

The Ku Klux Klan Kreed

We, the Order of the Knights of the Ku Klux Klan, reverentially acknowledge the majesty and supremacy of the Divine Being, and recognize the goodness and providence of the same.

We recognize our relation to the government of the United States of America, the supremacy of its constitution, the union of the states thereunder, and the constitution and laws thereof, and shall be devoted to the sublime principles of a pure Americanism and valiant in the defense of its ideals and its institutions.

We avow the distinction between the races of mankind, as same has been by the Creator, and we shall ever be true in the faithful maintenance of white separatism and will strenuously oppose any compromise thereof in any and all things.

We appreciate the intrinsic value of a real practical fraternal relationship among men and women of kindred thought, purpose and ideals and the infinite benefits accruable therefrom, and we shall faithfully devote ourselves to the practice of an honorable klanishness that the life and living of each may be a constant blessing to others.

"Non Silba Sed Anthar"
(Original Kreed Revised)

American Knights of the Ku Klux Klan
Order of Business

1. Opening Ceremony
2. Reading of approved minutes.
3. Reading of unapproved minutes or amendments.
4. Applications for Citizenship.
5. Recommendations.
6. Ceremony of Naturalization.
7. Does any klansman know of a klansman or a klansman's family who is in need of financial or fraternal assistance?
8. Reporting of standing or special committees.
9. Bills and communications.
10. Unfinished business.
11. General business.
12. Announcements.
13. Election and installation of officers.
14. For the good of the Order.
15. Payment of Klan dues or other indebtedness to the Klan.
16. Kligrapps statement of receipts and disbursements and their balances.
17. Reading and approving of minutes.
18. Closing ceremony.

List of Klan Officers With Explanation of Titles

National Imperial Wizard   (President)

Imperial Kladd   (Conducts Imperial Council Meetings, Acting Chairman of the Board, Personal Aid to the National Imperial Wizard)

Imperial Council   All Offices will be held by charter members or new inductees must meet a list of qualifications by the council.

Imperial Nighthawk   Due to the secretive nature of this branch of all offices National, State, County and their assistants will have a separate list of title explanations for their members.

Imperial Exalted Cyclops   is a combination of instructor, and guidance counselor for the county E.C.'s. He is responsible for the maintenance of the protocols of our Order and will have the unlimited power of controlling the State and County meetings, and National Public Meetings and all Klan functions that need protocol.

Grand Dragon Governor of the Realm (State)

State Hydra   Ass't to the G.D. Personal Bodyguard

Exalted Cyclops   The County Commissioner

Klaliff   Ass't to the E.C.

Imperial Klabee   National Treasurer (3 People acting as one)

Kilgrapp   Secretary to E.C.

The Klokann   Investigate applicants for membership (secretive)

Great Titan   Historian to the Order

(All officers are responsible for knowing their robe colors and stripes)

Imperial Decree

Subject: The Kloran

To: Exalted Cyclops and all Klansmen

Greetings:

Ever holding the best interest of the Invisible Empire, American Knight of the Ku Klux Klan, in mind and heart, and having had committed to me the sacred trust of its government; I therefore, by virtue of the authority vested in me, do decree and officially proclaim as follows:

The Kloran is "The Book" of the Invisible Empire, and is therefore a sacred book with our citizens and its contents must be rigidly safeguarded and its teachings honestly respected. The Book, or any part of it, must not be kept or carried where any person of the "alien" world may chance to become acquainted with its sacred contents as such. Its secrets must be held secure by you, and the prescribed "secret work" must be used only when necessary. No innovation will be tolerated, and frivolity or "horse-play" must not be allowed during any ceremony. All Klansmen are required to study and imbibe its wholesome teachings and morally profit thereby. All Klansmen are required to undergo an examination on the Kloran by the E.C. of his respective county, or another officer designated by him, before he can be an eligible applicant for knighthood. I hereby enjoin upon all E.C.s and their assistants to study carefully the Kloranic instructions given herein and to commit to memory especially their respective parts, and to demonstrate same in ceremony in a graceful, forceful and dignified manner. This decree is as binding as if its verbiage were incorporated in the Oath of Allegiance. In warning: A penalty sufficient will be speedily enforced for disregarding this decree in the profanation of the Kloran.

Done in the Aulice of his Majesty, the National Imperial Wizard, Emperor of the Invisible Empire, American Knights of the Ku Klux Klan.

American Knights of the Ku Klux Klan Klonklave

Just prior to the opening of the Klonklave, the Klaliff will procure the mounted flags and stand them at and in front of his station; the Klokard will procure the altar flag (Mioak) and the unsheathed sword and place the same on his station with flags folded compactly; the Klaliff will procure the vessel containing the dedication fluid and the Bible and put same on his station, and the Nighthawk will procure the fiery cross and stand it at and in front of the station of the Exalted Cyclops.

The time having arrived for the opening of the Klonklave, the E.C. (in his absence his substitute) will ascend his station, and standing, will give one rap with his gavel and say, "All present who have not attained citizenship in the Invisible Empire, American Knights of the Ku Klux Klan, will retire to the outer den under the escort of the nighthawk. The outer guard and inner guard will take their posts and faithfully guard the entrance to this Klavern."

* * * * * *

After all the applicants for citizenship shall have retired, the Klavern guards will close their respective doors, the outer guard making his secure. After this is done, no one will be allowed to pass into the Klavern until the Klonklave is duly opened. All substitute offices shall be appointed at this point. The E.C. will then give three raps with his gavel and take his seat. (The officers do not assume their stations at this time.) The E.C. will then command:

E.C. "The Klaliff of the Klan."

The Klaliff will advance to a point about five feet in front of the station of the E.C., salute and say:

Klaliff: "The Klaliff, Your Excellency!"

E.C. "You will ascertain with care if all present are Klansmen worthy to sit in the Klavern during the deliberations of this Klonklave."

Klaliff: "I have your orders, sir."

The Klaliff will then collect from each Klansman present the countersign and password. As he approaches a Klansman, that Klansman will whisper the words into the ear of the Klaliff and resume his seat immediately. If a Klansman should not have the words, he will remain standing. The Klaliff will proceed around the Klavern to all present. After he has finished, he will return to the E.C. and report as follows:

Klaliff: "Your Excellency: I respectfully report that all present are Klansmen worthy of the honor of sitting during the deliberations of this Klonklave." (If any present have not the words, the Klaliff will add to the above:) "Except those who stand before you; they presume to be Klansmen but they have not the words."

The E.C. will ascertain of the Kilgrapp if the ones standing are worthy; if so, he will instruct them to advance to his station and procure the same. If they are not worthy, all ceremony must cease until they become worthy or are ejected from the Klavern. If there be visiting Klansmen present, they must be invited to the E.C. station at this time, met by him, then faced toward the sacred altar and introduced to the Klan. All Klansmen will arise and give the visiting Klansmen TSOG. The visiting Klansmen will respond with TSOG. This done, the E.C. will give two raps with his gavel and say:

"My Unit Leaders, you will take your respective stations as your names are called."

The E.C., sitting in his station, will call the roll of his officers. When an officer's name is called, he will arise and answer: "Here", and proceed to his station, stand erect and face the sacred altar. (If an officer is absent his substitute will arise and call his own name and say: "Substitute," and then proceed to his station.) When the names of the Outer Guard and Nighthawk are called, the Inner Guard will answer for them if they are present, but if either of them or both of them should be absent, the *Inner Guard will give the names of their substitutes and so state.

No one will be allowed to sit on the station with an officer unless by consent of the E.C.

The E.C. will then arise. When he arises, the Unit Leaders will face him and salute; he will return the salute and charge them as follows:

"My unit Leaders: Your fellow Klansmen hold you in high esteem. You have been chosen to fill an important place in the affairs of this Klonklave and to set an example to all Klansmen of perfect observance of our oath and dutiful devotion to our great fraternity. Therefore, I charge you to discharge every duty incumbent upon you with dispatch, efficiency and dignity. Preserve peace and observe due decorum in our deliberations at this time, and preserve with honor in promoting and guarding well every interest of the Invisible Empire, American Knights of the Ku Klux Klan."

The E.C. will then give three raps and command:

E.C.: "My Unit Leaders and Klansmen, make ready!"

All will arise and put on their robes but leave their helmets off, and remain standing (robing may be omitted if there be no candidates in waiting, in the discretion of the E.C.). He will then say:

E.C. "Prepare the sacred altar."

The altar furnishings, having been previously placed, the Klokard will advance to the sacred altar from his station with altar flag (MIOAK) and sword; standing on side of altar next to the Klaliff's station, he will spread the flag across altar, and then place directly across center of altar the sword, with hilt toward the E.C., and takes position and faces the sacred altar.

As he leaves the sacred altar, the Klaliff will advance to the sacred altar with Bible and vessel of dedication fluid. Standing at point of sword, he will place the Bible, opened at the 12th Chapter of Romans, on and near the corner of sacred altar to his left and next to him, and the vessel of fluid on and near the corner of sacred altar to his right and opposite side from him, and takes position facing the sacred altar.

As he leaves the sacred altar, the nighthawk (in his absence, the Klokard) will advance to the sacred altar with the fiery cross and place it at and against center of sacred altar on side toward the E.C.'s station, light it, and take position facing the altar.

The Klokard, from his position, carefully surveys the sacred altar to make sure it is properly prepared, corrects any imperfections in its preparation, if any. From his position, faces the E.C. (the other three unit leaders will do likewise) and addresses the E.C. as follows:

Klokard: "Your Excellency, the sacred altar of the Klan is prepared; the fiery cross illuminates the Klavern."

E.C. "Faithful Klokard, why the fiery cross?"

Klokard: "Sir, it is the emblem of that sincere, unselfish devotion of all Klansmen, the sacred purpose and principles we have espoused."

E.C. "My Unit Leaders and Klansmen, what means the fiery cross?"

All: "We serve and sacrifice for the right."

E.C. "Klansmen all: you will gather for our opening devotions."

When he says this, he will arise and advance to and occupy the position, occupied by the Klaliff; as he approaches the Klaliff, that Unit Leader will advance to the Sacred Altar and take position near the point of the sword. All Klansmen will form on the quadrate, forming straight lines between these four positions. These four positions occupied by Unit Leaders form the corners of the Quadrate. The Unit Leaders, in taking these positions should step out far enough to accommodate the members between them, about an equal number on each side of quadrate. The distance between Klansmen in this quadrate must be about three feet. If there be more than enough to form one line, the others will form back of the first line and so on until all are in position. Great care must be exercised to form the quadrate correctly and symmetrically with the sacred altar in as near the exact center as possible.

The Klaliff will then, at the sacred altar, lead in the following prayer. (All must stand steady with heads bowed.)

"Our Father and our God, we, as Klansmen, acknowledge our dependence upon Thee and Thy loving kindness toward us; may our gratitude be full and constant and inspire us to walk in Thy ways.

"Give us to know that each Klansman by the process of thought and conduct, determine his own destiny, good or bad; may he forsake the bad and choose and strive for the good, remembering always that the Living Christ is a Klansman's criterion of character.

"Keep us in the blissful bonds of fraternal union, of clannish fidelity one toward another, loyalty to this our great institution. Give us to know that the crowning glory of a Klansman is to serve. Harmonize our souls with the sacred principles and purposes of our noble Order that we may keep our sacred oath inviolate, as Thou art our witness.

"Bless those absent from our gathering at this time; Thy peace be in their hearts and homes.

"God save our nation! and help us to be a nation worthy of existence on the earth. Keep ablaze in each Klansman's heart the sacred fire of a devoted patriotism to our country and its government.

"We invoke Thy blessing upon our Emperor, the National Imperial Wizard, and his official family, in the administration of the affairs pertaining to the government of the Invisible Empire. Grant him wisdom and grace, and may each Klansman's heart and soul be inclined toward him in loving loyalty and unwavering devotion.

"Oh God! For Thy glory and our good, we humbly ask these things in the Name of Him who taught us to serve and sacrifice for the right. Amen!" (All say, "Amen!")

After the prayer, facing the sacred altar, all will give together TSOG and holding same will say, "For my country, the Klan, my fellow Klansmen and my home." Then all give the white power salute to the flag. The E.C. then immediately returns to his station; as he vacates his position, the Klaliff will advance from the sacred altar and occupy this position; as the E.C. steps into his station, faces the assembly, and gives one rap with the gavel. At this, each Klansman will face him and give TSOTF-C, then TSPC-1, then raise TSOS, and the TSOK-C; as he responds with TSPK-C they will recover. He holds TSOK-C and says:

"My Unit Leaders and Klansmen: In the sacred cause we have entered, be thou faithful unto death; be patriotic toward our country; be clannish toward Klansmen; be devoted to our great fraternity."

He then recovers TSOK-C, and says: "My Unit Leaders and Klansmen: What is the sworn duty of a Klansman in Klonklave assembled?"

All answer in unison: "To maintain peace and harmony in all the deliberations of the Klan in Klonklave assembled, and take heed to instructions given."

The E.C. will then give two raps with his gavel. After all are seated he will say:

E.C. "I will now officially proclaim that this Klonklave of _____ Klan Unit #_____Realm of _____ of the Invisible Empire, American Knights of the Ku Klux Klan, duly opened for the dispatch of business."

E.C. "Faithful Inner Guard: You may now admit all qualified Klansmen, but guard well the portal to this Klavern. The nighthawk (in his absence, the Klaliff) will extinguish the fiery cross."

Closing Ceremony

The order of business having been finished, the E.C. will arise, give on rap with his gavel and say:

"My Unit Leaders and Klansmen: The sacred purpose of the gathering of the Klan at this time has been fulfilled; the deliberations of this Klonklave have ended."

E.C.: "Faithful Klaliff: What is the four-fold duty of a Klansman?"

The Klaliff will arise and say:

Klaliff: "To worship God; be patriotic toward our country; be devoted and loyal to our Emperor, and to practice clannishness toward his fellow Klansmen." (and remains standing).

E.C.: "Faithful Klaliff: How speaketh the oracles of our God?"

Klaliff: "Thou shalt worship the Lord Thy God,. Render unto the things which are the states. Love the brotherhood. Honor the King. Bear ye one another's burdens, and so fulfill the law of Christ." (All remain standing.

E.C.: "Faithful Klokard: What does a Klansman value more than life?"

The Klokard will rise and say:

Klokard: "Honor to a Klansman is more than life." (and remains standing).

E.C. "Faithful Klaliff: How is a Klansman to preserve his honor?"

Klaliff: "By the discharge of duty in the faithful keeping of his oath." (All remain standing).

All the other officers will arise and say in unison:

Officers: "Your Excellency: The immaculate truth has been spoken." (and remain standing.)

E.C. "What say you, my fellow Klansmen?"

All members will arise and say, in unison:

Members: "Amen!" (and remain standing.)

E.C.: "My terrors and Klansmen: You know well the duty of a Klansman; be thou not recreant to duty's demands as we go hence from this Klavern to enter the stressful struggle of the alien world. Protect your honor by keeping inviolate your sacred oath."

The E.C. then gives one rap with his gavel, and gives the SOK-C together.

E.C. "The crowning glory of a Klansman is to serve, (non silba sed anthar)".

All will say: "Not for self, but for others. Let us be faithful in serving our God, our Country, our Emperor and our fellow Klansmen."

The E.C. will then give one rap with his gavel and say:

E.C. "My faithful Klansmen: As peace dwells among us, you will assemble for our parting devotions."

All will assemble on the quadrate formed as in opening ceremony (the inner guard and outer guard making secure their respective doors). The Klaliff stands at the sacred altar. All will stand facing the sacred altar and come tot he SOTF-C and resting palms on back of each other, thus paralleling the ARS, and will join in singing the following closing clode: - All Standing.

"Blest be the Klansman's tie of real fraternal love,
That binds us in a fellowship akin to that above."

Each will stand with left hand over the heart and the right resting on the left shoulder of the Klansman to the right.

E.C. "Klansmen: United in the sacred bond of clanish fidelity, we stand, but divided by selfishness and strife, we fall; shall we stand or shall we fall?"

All will answer: "We will stand; for our blood is not pledged in vain."

Each Klansman will look toward the mounted flag and will give the sign of prayer and then stand with bowed heads; the Klaliff standing at the sacred altar will pronounce the following benediction:

The Benediction

"May the blessings of our God wait upon thee and the sun of glory shine around thy head: may the gates of plenty, honor, and happiness be always open to thee and thine so far as they will not rob thee of eternal joys.

"May no strife disturb thy days, nor sorrow distress thy nights. And when death shall summons thy departure may the Savior's blood have washed thee from all impurities, perfected thy initiation, and thus prepared, enter thou into the Empire Invisible and repose thy soul in perpetual peace. Amen!"

All say: "Amen!"

The benediction having been pronounced, the E.C. will immediately return to his station, give one rap with his gavel and say:

E.C. "I now officially proclaim that this Klonklave of _____ Klan Unit # _____Realm of _____of the Invisible Empire, American Knights of the Ku Klux Klan, duly closed. The Klan will gather again in (regular or special) Klonklave _____night."

E.C. "Klansmen, one and all."

Saying this, he LTSOS, which all will do likewise. All will then give and hold TSPG, and the E.C. will say:

E.C.: "To you, faithful Klansmen, goodnight!"

All will say: Your Excellency, good night!"

He and they will recover TSPG together. The E.C. gives one rap and announces: "The Klaliff and the nighthawk will gather and make secure the properties of the Klan. The Klan is dismissed. Faithful Inner Guard: You will open the portal that all Klansman may pass to the outer world."

On going out, each Klansman must see to it that the robe and helmet worn by him is carefully and properly placed in locker or other place for safe keeping, if he does not carry same home with him by permission of the E.C.

Let it be known that from the old days came the "Invisible Empire." Now that we are in the wicked modern times of the Fourth Rebirth of the Klan, the American Knights of the Ku Klux Klan, use the "Invisible Empire" term strictly out of respect and nostalgia for the days gone by of the 1915 Rebirth of the Klan.

The American Knights also respect the old ways of naturalization, but we do allow our Klavern E.C.s to "do their own thing" when it comes to this most sacred of sacred ceremonies. The following is a revision of the 1915 naturalization ceremony....

NATURLIZATION CEREMONY
AMERICAN KNIGHTS OF THE KU KLUX KLAN

When the Ceremony of Naturalization shall have been reached in the regular order of business, the Inner Guard will signal by ALLW to the Outer Guard, who will repeat the signal to the Nighthawk in the outer den with candidates. Prior to the signal, the Nighthawk will have presented a blank petition of citizenship to each candidate, requesting him to read and sign name. (Said petition to be witnessed by the Nighthawk). He will collect from each candidate the Klectoken, if same has been previously paid. On hearing the signal of the Outer Guard, he will approach the outer door of the inner den and give thereon seven raps. (Having in his possession the petition of the candidates and the klectokens by him collected).

Outer Guard: "Who dares to approach so near the entrance to this Klavern?"

Nighthawk: "The Nighthawk of the Klan."

Outer Guard: "Advance with the countersign." (The NH will then give the countersign in a low whisper through the wicket.)

Outer Guard: (will open the outer door and say) "Pass".

The NH passes the outer door into the inner den of the Klavern and at once enrobes completely and then approaches and signals on the inner door. The Inner Guard will open the wicket. When the wicket is open the NH will GALLW.

Inner Guard: "Who seeks entrance to the Klavern?"

NH: "The Nighthawk of the Klan with important information and documents from the alien world for his Excellency."

The Inner Guard secures the wicket, salutes and reports to the E.C.

Inner Guard: "Your Excellency: The Nighthawk of the Klan is respectfully waiting to enter the Klavern with information and documents from the alien world."

E.C.: "You will permit him to enter."

Inner Guard: (Through the wicket GALLW, which is answered by the NH with ALLW, and gives the password through the wicket). Then the Inner Guard opens the door and says: "You have His excellency's permission to enter." The NH enters, steps across the threshold of the Klavern, stands erect and GTSOG; all will answer by the same from their seats. The NH will then proceed to altar. Arriving at the altar, he GTNH, then GTSOF-C. Then removes his helmet and GTSOK-C. and stands erect and steady.

E.C.: "Faithful Nighthawk. You may now speak and impart to us the important information in your possession."

NH: (bows and speaks): "Your Excellency: Sir, pursuant to my duty in seeking laudable adventure in the alien world, I found these men (here he gives their names). They having read the Imperial Proclamation of our Emperor, and prompted by unselfish motives, desire a nobler life. In consequence, they have made the honorable decision to forsake the world or selfishness and fraternal alienation and emigrate to the delectable bounds of the Invisible Empire and become loyal citizens of the same."

E.C. "Faithful Nighthawk: This is indeed important information, and most pleasant to hear. Important, in that it evidences human progress; most pleasant, in that it reveals through you a Klansman's sincere appreciation of his sacred mission among men and his fidelity to duty in the betterment of mankind. Their respective petitions will be received and justly considered."

NH: (bows and says): "Sir, I have in my possession the required petitions for citizenship of the men named, together with their klectoken."

E.C.: "Then you will approach and deliver same to the Kligrapp who will publish them to all Klansmen in Klonklave assembled."

(The NH will deliver the petitions and klectokens to the Kligrapp and resume his position at the altar. The Kligrapp will then arise and publish the names of the petitioners and hand the petitioners to the E.C. and resume his seat. The E.C. will say:

E.C.: "Klansmen, you have heard the publication of the petition for citizenship in the Invisible Empire of (here he gives the names). Does any Klansman, on his oath of allegiance, know of any just reason why these aliens, or any of them, should be denied citizenship in the Invisible Empire?"

(If there be no objections, the E.C. will address the Nighthawk.)

E.C.: "Faithful Nighthawk, you will inform these alien petitioners from me: 'That it is the constant disposition of a Klansman to assist those who aspire to things noble in thought and conduct, and to extend a helping hand to the worthy; that their desires are sincerely respected, their manly petitions are being seriously considered in the light of justice and honor. With true faith, a man may expect a just answer to his prayers, and his virtuous hopes will ultimately ripen into a sublime fruition."

The Nighthawk bows and says: "I have your orders, sir," and retires to the outer door of the inner den of the Klavern and through the wicket of the outer door, informs the candidates as follows:

NH: "Worthy aliens: His Excellency, the Exalted Cyclops, being the direct representative of his Majesty, our Emperor, and chief guardian of the portal of the Invisible Empire, has officially instructed me to inform you that it is the constant disposition of a Klansman to assist those who aspire to things noble in thought and conduct, and to extend a helping hand to the worthy. Therefore, your desires are sincerely respected and your manly petitions are being seriously considered in the light of justice and honor. With true faith, you may expect a just answer to your prayers, and your virtuous hopes will ultimately ripen into a sublime fruition. This is the decision of His Excellency, the Exalted Cyclops, with all his Klan concurring."

The Nighthawk returns to his station in the Klavern without form.

E.C.: Faithful Klaliff: You will examine under witness the alien petitioners, as to their qualifications."

The Klaliff, with his assistants, retire to the outer den and will propound to the candidates in waiting the following required 'Qualifying Interrogatories' and then immediately administer sections 1 and 2 of the "Oath of Allegiance", require each candidate to place his right hand over his heart and raise his left hand to heaven.

Qualifying Interrogatories

The Klokard will first ask each candidate his name and then speak to the candidates in the outer den as follows:

"Sirs: The American Knights of the Ku Klux Klan, as a great and essentially patriotic fraternal, benevolent order, does not discriminate against a man on account of his religious or political creed, when same does not conflict with or antagonize the sacred rights and privileges guaranteed by our government and Christian ideals and institutions.

"Therefore, to avoid any misunderstanding, and as evidence that we do not seek to impose unjustly the requirements of this Order upon anyone who cannot, on account of his religious or political scruples, voluntarily meet our requirements and faithfully practice our principles, and as proof that we respect all honest men in their sacred convictions, whether same are agreeable with our requirements or not, we require as an absolute necessity on the part of each you an affirmative answer to each of the following questions:

The 10 questions follow.

The 1st and 2nd Sections of the Oath are administered.

This done, he, with his assistants, will return to the sacred altar. He will salute and report as follows: "Your Excellency: (Here state the number of petitioners)____men in waiting have each duly qualified to enter our Klavern to journey through the mystic cave in quest of citizenship in the Invisible Empire."

E.C. "The Klaliff of the Klan!" The Klaliff will arise and advance to a position immediately in front of the E.C., and about five feet from his station, and salute and say:

Klaliff: "The Klaliff, Your Excellency!"

E.C. "You will retire under special orders to the outer premises of the Klavern, assume charge of the worthy aliens in waiting, and afford them a safe journey from the world of selfishness and fraternal alienation to the sacred altar of the Empire of chivalry, industry, honor and love."

Klaliff salutes the E.C. and says: "I have your orders, sir!"

He retired to the room where the candidates are, lines them up in single file, the left hand of the rear man on the left shoulder of the man in front. He then takes his place in front of them and says: "Follow me and be men (or a man)!" He proceeds to the outer door of the inner den. Outer Guard (opens the wicket and says): "Who and what is your business?"

Klaliff: "I am the Klaliff of Klan No._____Realm of _____, acting under special orders of His Excellency, our Exalted Cyclops; I am in charge of a party!"

Outer Guard: "What be the nature of your party?"

Klaliff: "Worthy aliens from the world of selfishness and fraternal alienation prompted by unselfish motive, desire the honor of citizenship in the Invisible Empire and the fellowship of the Klansmen."

Outer Guard: "Has your party been selected with care?"

Klaliff: "These men (or this man) are (or is) known and vouched for by Klansmen in Klonklave assembled."

Outer Guard: "Have they (or has he) the marks?"

Klaliff: "The distinguishing marks of a Klansman are not found in the fibre of his garments or his social or financial standing, but are spiritual; a chivalric head, a compassionate heart, a prudent tongue and a courageous will, all devoted to our country, our homes and each other. These are distinguishing marks of a Klansman, oh Faithful Outer Guard! And these men claim the marks."

Outer Guard: "What if one of your party should prove himself to be a traitor?"

Klaliff: "He would be immediately banished in disgrace from the Invisible Empire without fear or favor; conscience would tenaciously torment him, remorse would repeatedly revile him, and direful things would befall him."

Outer Guard: "Do they (or does he) know all this?"

Klaliff: "All this he (or they) now know. He (or they) has (or have) heard, and they must heed."

Outer Guard: "Faithful Klaliff: You speak the truth."

Klaliff: "Faithful Outer Guard, a Klansman speaketh the truth in and from his heart. A lying scoundrel may wrap his disgraceful frame within the sacred folds of Klansman's robe and deceive the very elect, but only a Klansman possesses a Klansman's heart and a Klansman's soul.

Outer Guard: "Advance with the countersign."

The Klaliff advances and whispers the countersign through the wicket to the Outer Guard.

Outer Guard (opens the door and says): "With heart and soul, I, the Outer Guard of the Klan, welcome you and open the way for you to attain the most noble achievement in your earthly career. Be faithful and true unto death and all will be well and your reward will be sure. Noble Klaliff, pass with your party!"

The Klaliff, with his party, will pass the outer door and stop. He will give ALLW. The Inner Guard, upon hearing the LLW, will announce:

"Inner Guard: "Your Excellency and Klansmen assembled: I hear from the watch the signals of the Klaliff of the Klan with a party!"

* * * * *

E.C. "My Unit Leaders and Klansmen, one and all: Make ready!"

Each Klansman present will put on his helmet, both aprons dropped down, robes completely buttoned and girdles tied and capes adjusted. All lights must be turned down so as to make the Klavern almost dark. All must remain as still and as quiet as possible. There must be no moving, talking or noise — only as the ceremony requires. Striking matches and smoking during the ceremony is absolutely forbidden. If an officer has to read, he must use an electric or battery flashlight, and throw the light only on the page he is reading. When all are ready, the Inner Guard will answer the signal of the Klaliff with ALLW and begin to OTDS.

Klaliff (On STDOS the Klaliff will say to his party): "Sirs, the portal of the Invisible Empire is being opened for you. Your righteous prayer is being answered and you have found favor in the sight of the Exalted Cyclops and his Klansmen assembled. Follow me and be prudent."

As the Klaliff approaches the threshold of the inner door with his party, the Inner Guard will stop them by facing them with TSOF-C. He will then recover TSOF-C, face inward and stand erect and steady. (The Klaliff, or person selected, just previous to this has stationed himself near the door where he can be heard by the candidates but not seen by them.)

Klaliff: "God give us men! The Invisible Empire demands strong minds, great hearts, true faith and ready hands - Men whom the lust of offices does not kill; men whom the spoils of office cannot buy; men who possess opinions and a will; men who have honor; men who will not lie; men who can stand before a demagogue, and damn his treacherous flatteries without winking! Tall men, sun-crowned, who live above the fog; in public duty and in private thinking; for while the rabble, with their thumb-worn creeds, their large professions and their little deeds, mingle in selfish strife, lo! freedom weeps; men who serve not for selfish booty, but real men - courageous, who flinch not at duty; men of dependable character; men of sterling worth. Then wrongs will be redressed, and right will rule the earth. God give us Men!"

After a pause, the Inner Guard faces the candidates and says:

Inner Guard: "Sirs, will you (or each of you) by your daily life as Klansmen earnestly endeavor to be an answer to this prayer?"

He then faces the E.C. and says:

Inner Guard: "Your Excellency and fellow Klansmen: Just such men are (just such a man is) standing without the portal of the Invisible Empire, desiring the lofty honor of citizenship therein, and ready and willing to unflinchingly face every duty on them (or him) imposed."

* * * * *

E.C.: "Faithful Inner Guard and Klansmen: Let him (them) enter the Klavern in quest of citizenship, but keep you a Klansman's eye of scrutiny upon him (them). And if he (one of them) should flinch a duty or show himself a cowardly weakling or a treacherous scalawag, at this time or in the future, it will be your sworn duty to eject him (them) from the portal of the Invisible Empire without fear or favor and do so without delay. Be thou not recreant to duty's demands!"

(While the above prayer is being said the Nighthawk takes the fiery cross from the altar, lights it and takes a position immediately in front of and about four feet from the Klaliff's station. Facing the Inner Guard, holding the fiery cross above his head.)

Inner Guard: (Steps aside and says to the Klaliff): "Pass".

(When the Klaliff crosses the threshold of the Klavern, he will stop and give TSOG. All Klansmen, except the station officers, will arise, face the Klaliff and give TSOG. Then face the altar and remain standing with TSOC-I. The Klaliff will then proceed with his party toward the Nighthawk. As the Klaliff approaches the Nighthawk with his party and gets within about six feet of him, the Nighthawk will about face and march in front of the Klaliff about six feet from him on the journey. Until he is halted by the signal ALLS from the E.C. When he hears the signal, he will stop his party. Answer the signal with ALLW, then face his party toward the sacred altar. When this is done, the Nighthawk, with the fiery cross, takes a position in front of and about six feet from the party, facing the party with the cross uplifted. He remains in this position until he hears the second signal of ALLW from the E.C. when he will resume his position at the head of the party in front of the Klaliff and move on. When the Klaliff hears the second signal, he will face his party as they were, answer the signal with ALLW and follow the Nighthawk.

(When the first signal of ALLW of the E.C. is given, all Klansmen, except the station officers, Inner and Outer Guards, will form from their seats, march around the hall in single file. The Inner Guard leading to his right, pass in front along the line of the party, between the party and the Nighthawk, each Klansman will look the party squarely in the eyes, but continue moving. After passing the party the Klaliff will form the Klansmen in a double line with open ranks about six feet apart and facing each other. Holding TSOC-I, and standing steady on the opposite side of the Klavern, the E.C. then gives the second signal of ALLW. The Nighthawk will lead the Klaliff and his party on their journey by way of the E.C. station and through the formation of Klansmen. All this must be done quietly, with dignity and with a steady pace.

(After the Klaliff and his party shall have passed, the formation of Klansmen will without signal return to their seats, but remain standing until the Klaliff presents his party to the E.C.; then they quietly sit down.

(As the Inner Guard approaches the station of the Klaliff after he has passed the formation of Klansmen, the Klaliff will arise and GTSOG and halt him with same. The Nighthawk also stops.)

Klaliff: "Who are you that walk in the Klavern at this hour?"

Inner Guard: "The Inner Guard of the Klan with a party whom the eye of the Unknown has seen and doth constantly observe."

Klaliff: "What be the nature of your party?"

Inner Guard: "Faithful Klaliff: These are men. (or This is a man) as the Invisible Empire and a time like this demands - Men (A man) of strong minds (mind)., great heart(s), true faith and ready hands, worthy aliens known and vouched for by Klansmen in Klonklave assembled, and by order of His Excellency. I, the Inner Guard of the Klan, am their (or his) guide to the sacred altar.

Klaliff: "Pass on!"

(The journey from entrance of the Klavern to the E.C. station must be made in a circle around the Klavern.)

The Nighthawk will move on, followed by the Inner Guard with his party and will then continue his journey until he arrives at the station of the E.C., when he shall stop and line his company up in a straight line immediately in front of the station. The Nighthawk stops, but does not change position. The Inner Guard steps to the rear of his party and will address the E.C. as follows:

Inner Guard: "Your Excellency: Sir, pursuant to your order, I present to you these (or this) alien aspirants, men (or man) of dependable character and courage, who aspire(s) to the noble life and the high honor of citizenship in the Invisible Empire."

The Exalted Cyclops will arise and address the candidates as follows:

E.C. "It is indeed refreshing to meet face to face with men (or a man) like you, who actuated by manly motives, aspire to all things noble for yourselves and humanity.

"The luster of the holy light of chivalry has lost its former glory and is sadly dimmed by the choking dust of selfish, sordid gain. Pass on!"

The E.C. will resume his seat, and the Inner Guard will face his party toward the Nighthawk and advance behind the Nighthawk until he hears the signal of ALLW from the Klaliff. On hearing the signal from the Klaliff the Nighthawk stops and stands steady. The Inner Guard will stop his party immediately in front of the Klaliff's station and face them to the Klaliff's station and answer the signal by the same. On receiving the answer, the Klaliff will arise and address the party as follows:

Klaliff: "Real fraternity, by shameful neglect, has been starved until so weak her voice is lost in the courts of her own castle, and she passes unnoticed by her sworn subjects as she moves along the crowded streets and through the din of the market place, man's valuation of man is by the standard of wealth and not worth. Selfishness is the festive queen among human kind and multitudes forget honor, justice, love and God and every religious conviction to do homage to her,. and yet with the cruel heart of Jezebel, she slaughters the souls of thousands of her devotees daily. Pass on!"

The Klaliff will continue to address the party as follows:

"The unsatiated thirst for gain is dethroning reason and judgment in the citadel of the human soul. And men maddened thereby, forget their patriotic, domestic and social obligations and duties, and fiendishly fight for a place in the favor of the goddess of glittering gold. They starve their own souls and make sport of spiritual development. Pass on!"

The Klaliff will face his party as before, and advance behind the Nighthawk until he hears the signals of ALLW from the E.C. On hearing the signal of the E.C. the Nighthawk stops and goes to and takes party immediately in front of the E.C.'s station. Facing them to the E.C. and then answers the signal with the same. On receiving the party, the E.C. addresses them as follows:

E.C.: "Sirs, we congratulate you on your manly decision to forsake the world of selfishness and fraternal alienation and emigrate to the delectable bounds of the Invisible Empire and become loyal citizens of the same. The prime purpose of this great Order is to develop character clanishness, to protect the home and the chastity of womanhood and to exemplify a pure patriotism towards our glorious country.

"You as citizens of the Invisible Empire must be actively patriotic toward our country and constantly clanish towards Klansmen socially, physically, morally and vocationally. Will you assume this obligation of citizenship?......

"Sirs: If you have any doubt as to your ability to qualify, either in body or character, as citizens of the Invisible Empire, you now have an opportunity to retire from this place with the goodwill of the Klan to attend you. For I warn you now, if you falter or fail at this time or in the future as a Klansman, in Klonklave or in life, you will be banished from citizenship in the Invisible Empire without fear or favor.

"This is a serious undertaking. We are not here to make sport of you, nor indulge in the silly frivolity of circus clowns. Be you well assured that 'He that putteth his hands to the plow and looketh back is not fit for the kingdom of heaven,' or worthy of the high honor of citizenship in the Invisible Empire, or the fervent fellowship of Klansmen. Don't deceive yourselves; you cannot deceive us and we will not be mocked. Do you wish to retire?.............

"Faithful Klaliff, you will direct the way for these worthy aliens to the sacred altar of the Empire of chivalry, honor, industry and love, on order that they may make further progress toward attaining citizenship in the Invisible Empire, American Knights of the Ku Klux Klan."

The Klaliff will conduct his party to the sacred altar by way of his station.

When he has arrived within about six feet of the station, he will turn, square to his left and continue in a straight direction until he reaches a point about six feet of the sacred altar toward the station of the Exalted Cyclops; he will then turn square to his right and continue until he has passed the sacred altar about four feet; he will turn square to his left and continue until he passes the sacred altar bout six feet, when he will turn square to his left and bring his party into the formation of a three-quarter hollow square, and will face them towards the sacred altar.

(If he has five candidates or a fewer number he will form them in a straight line facing the altar on the side of the altar toward the Klaliff's station and about four feet from the altar, and then perfect the three-quarter hollow square formation with Klansmen.)

The Nighthawk takes his place with the fiery cross held aloft just from the corner of the sacred altar to the right of the E.C. He stands within the quadrate. The fiery cross is held aloft during the administering of the oath and dedicatory ceremony.

The first paragraph above gives a general idea regarding the journey of the candidates to the sacred altar, as to turning angles and as to distances, etc. In making this journey the number of candidates and the good judgment of the Klaliff will determine the size of the hollow square formation and the best results in getting to and forming it.

The Klaliff should study well his part in the floor work for his is very important and an impressive part. He should exercise good military mannerisms in his work.

When the Klaliff has perfected the three-quarter hollow square formation, he will advance to the point about midway between the altar and the station of the Exalted Cyclops, salute and in a strong, clear voice say:

Klaliff: "Your excellency: The aliens in our midst from the world of selfishness and fraternal alienation, forsake the past and are now ready and willing to bind themselves by an unyielding tie to the Invisible Empire, American Knights of the Ku Klux Klan."

Then the Klaliff will about face and advance to his position opposite of the center and to the rear of the line of candidates toward his station, and await orders.

The E.C. with his assistant, will, with steady pace, form across the open side of the hollow square so as to complete the square, and will administer Sections III and IV of the Oath of Allegiance. (Please note that if the Grand Dragon is visiting the Klonklave assembly, he will be administering the Oath of Allegiance in its entire capacity, depending on whether or not there are officers to be naturalized). The E.C. stands between his assistant, after the oath shall have been administered. The Klaliff will about face and advance to a point about midway between the altar and salute and address the E.C. thus:

Klaliff: "Your Excellency: the worthy aspirants at the sacred altar of the Klan have each voluntarily assumed, without mental reservation, the solemn and thrice binding Oath of Allegiance to the Invisible Empire, American Knights of the Ku Klux Klan, and are waiting to be dedicated to the holy service of our country, the Klan, each other, our homes and humanity."

E.C.: "Faithful Klaliff, you and your assistants have performed your duty well; now you may rest, but stand by in readiness to perform other duties, if such arise."

The Klaliff resumes his place in the quadrate formation between his assistants. The E.C. then proceeds to the sacred altar to perform the following ceremony of dedication.

Dedication

The E.C. addresses the candidates as follows:

E.C.: "Sirs: Have (each of) you assumed without mental reservation your Oath of Allegiance to the Invisible Empire?

"Mortal man cannot assume a more binding oath: character and courage alone will enable you to keep it. Always remember that to keep this oath means to you honor, happiness and life; but to violate it means disgrace, dishonor and death. May honor, happiness and life be yours."

* * * * *

(Then he holds up the vessel from the sacred altar, containing the dedication fluid and addresses the candidates as follows:)

E.C.: "With this transparent life-giving, powerful God-given fluid, more precious and far more significant than all the sacred oils of the ancients, I set you (or each of you) apart from the men of your daily association, to the greater and honorable task you have voluntarily allotted yourselves, citizens of the Invisible Empire, American Knights of the Ku Klux Klan.

"As a Klansman, may your character be as transparent, your life purpose as powerful, your motive in all things as magnanimous and as pure, and your clanishness as real and as faithful as the manifold drops herein, and you a vital being as useful to humanity as is pure water to mankind.

"Sirs: 'Neath the uplifted fiery cross which by its holy light looks down upon you to bless with its sacred traditions of the past, I dedicate you in body, mind, in spirit and in life, to the holy service of our country, our Klan, our homes, each other and humanity."

The E.C. advances to the candidates and pours a few drops of the dedication fluid on each candidate's back and says: "In body," pours a few drops on his head and says: "In mind," says: "In spirit." Then moves his hand in a horizontal circular motion around the candidate's head and says: "and in life." After his he says: "Thus dedicated by us, now consecrate yourselves to the sacred cause you have entered.

(To all he will say): "My Unit Leaders and Klansmen: Let us pray."

(All except those officiating at the sacred altar must kneel. The E.C. will step back to the rear and left of the Klaliff; the Nighthawk remains in his position; the chaplain will advance and stand to the Exalted Cyclops, and will use the following:

Dedication Prayer

"God of all, Author of all good, Thou who didst create man and do so propose that man should fill a distinct place and perform a specific work in the economy of they good government, Thou hast revealed Thyself and Thy purpose to man, and by this revelation we have learned our place and our work. Therefore, we have solemnly dedicated ourselves as Klansmen to that sublime work harmonic with Thy will and purpose in our creation.

"Now, oh God! We, through Thy goodness, have here dedicated with Thine own divinely distilled fluid these manly men at the altar kneeling, who have been moved by worthy motives and impelled by noble impulses to turn from selfishness and fraternal alienation, and to espouse with body, mind, spirit and life, the holy service of our country, our Klan, our home and each other, - we beseech Thee to dedicate them with the fullness of Thy Spirit. Keep him (or each of them) true to his (or their) sacred solemn oath to our noble cause. To the glory of Thy great Name. Amen!" (All say, "Amen!")

Immediately after the prayer all will arise. The E.C. will step to the altar and instruct the candidates to rise. The chaplain will step back to his place.

* * * * *

The E.C. will address the candidates as follows:

E.C. "Sirs (or Sir): You are no longer strangers or aliens among us, but are citizens with us; and with confidence in your character that have not sworn falsely or deceitfully in the assumption of your oath, I, on behalf of our Emperor, National Imperial Wizard, Grand Dragon, Realm_____and all Klansmen, welcome you to the citizenship in the Empire of chivalry, honor, industry and love."

After saying this, the E.C. will raise the front apron of his helmet (and all Klansmen will do the same) and as a token of welcome he will greet each of the candidates with TSOK, and then return to his position at the altar and says:

E.C. "By authority vested in me by our Emperor, National Imperial Wizard, Grand Dragon of the Realm, American Knights of the Ku Klux Klan, and invest you with the title of 'Klansman,' the most honorable title among men."

This done, the E.C. returns to his station and the candidate or candidates are greeted under the fiery cross by all Klansmen with TSOK, the Klaliff leading the line.

This done, the Nighthawk will extinguish the fiery cross and replace it at the alter and take his seat. The Inner Guard will have turned on the lights of the Klavern. This done, the E.C. will say:

E.C. "The Klaliff of the Klan."

The Klaliff will advance from his position at the rear of the candidates to a point above five feet in front of the E.C. and salute and say:

Klaliff: "The Klaliff, your Excellency."

E.C. "You will escort the Klansmen at the sacred altar to your station that they may receive instructions in the way of the Klavern."

Klaliff: (The Klaliff will salute and say): "I have your orders, sir!"

The Klaliff conducts the candidates and forms them in a straight line in front where seats have been provided and will instruct them to be seated. He will take a position at the center and to the rear of the candidates and remain standing while the instructions are being given.

The Way of the Klavern

You will approach the outer door of the inner den and give thereon one rap and strike the O. The Outer Guard will answer the same. He will open the wicket and you will GASLW. He will say, "Who are you?" You will give him your name as Klansman_____, giving the name, number and realm of your Klan. He will say: "Advance and give the countersign." You will advance and whisper the countersign through the wicket. If you are qualified to enter he will open the door and say to you, "Pass."

You will pass into the inner den and say:"Outer Guard, what of the night?" If there be candidates to be initiated or already present, he will say, "Strangers are near; be prudent!" On hearing this, you will completely enrobe before entering the Klavern. But if there be no candidates, and no initiatory work to be done, "All are known." Hearing this you will not robe, but enter as you are.
* * * * * *

You will then approach the inner door and give thereon **** You will then strike the F.C.; at this the Inner Guard will open the wicket and say: "Who is it, and what is your business?" You will answer: "I am Klansman_____; I seek entrance to the Klavern to meet with my fellows." If necessary, he will demand your receipt or ascertain of the Kligrapp if you are entitled to enter; if so, he will then open the wicket and say, "Password." If the same is correct, he will open the door and say, "Pass Klansman."

You will pass clear of the door. Stop. Stand erect and GTSOG and hold same until someone answers it. Then pass on to the sacred altar, face the station of the E.C., then face the mounted flag and GTNH. Then face the E.C. and GTSOF-C; then raise RSOS if you are not robed you will remove your helmet instead of raising

TSOS; the GTSOK-C which will be answered by the Exalted Cyclops with TSOR; you then will take your seat. If you are robed and others have their helmets on disguised, you will not remove your helmet, but will take your seat without disclosing your identity. If the Exalted Cyclops is engaged, you will give TSOK-C to the Klaliff.

To retire from the Klavern while same is in session, you will advance to the sacred altar, face the Exalted Cyclops and lower TSOS, or put on your helmet; then GTSOK-C; if he answers you with TSPG, you may retire. If the Exalted Cyclops does not answer you, you must raise TSOS and return to your seat. On going out of the Klavern you must remove and conceal your robe and helmet in the inner den of the Klavern.

During the deliberations of the Klonklave, if you wish to talk to the assembly, make a motion, or even second a motion, you must arise to your feet, then address the Exalted Cyclops by saying: "Your Excellency," and touch your forehead with the ends of the fingers of your right hand. If he recognizes you, turn the palm of your right hand toward him and drop your hand. Then you may speak. He will recognize you by looking at you and saying, Klansman. If he does not recognize you readily, then drop your hand and resume your seat, and later try again. No man will be in order unless he gets recognition of the Exalted Cyclops by addressing him thusly.

The gavel is the emblem of authority of the Exalted Cyclops, and its signals must be rigidly respected. Any disrespect shown the Exalted Cyclops during a Klonklave is an insult to the entire Klan which he serves, and an affront to our Emperor, National Imperial Wizard, Grand Dragon who he represents in their official capacity. The entire Klan is under direct obligations to command due respect from any and all without fear or favor.

One rap of the gavel calls for silence, and attention, whether you stand or sit.

Two raps of the gavel calls for silence and to seats.

Three raps of the gavel call — all to feet.

Remember all.........are given with the LH & A only, when B arte not required.

V-S-A.

V-S-N.

S-O-G (same is used for S-O-R).

S-O-K-C.

S-O-KLS.

S-O-F-C.

S-O-P.

A-T-S-O-P.

S-O-S.

A-T-S-O-S.

K-S.

N-H.

T-K-O-K.

THE KLONVERSATION

After the instructions have been given, the Klaliff will say:

"I will now conduct you to the Exalted Cyclops where you will receive from him the CS and PW. The Sacred Symbol, and Imperial instructions to which give earned heed."

The Klaliff conducts the party to the station of the E.C. and says:

"Your Excellency: These Klansmen (or this Klansman) having been instructed in the Way of the Klavern, now await to receive from you the CS and PW. The Sacred Symbol of the Klan and Imperial instructions."

E.C.: (will arise and say): "The insignia or mark of a Klansman is honor all secrets and secret information of the Invisible Empire as committed to you on your honor. A Klansman values honor more than life itself. Be true to honor. Then to all the world you will be true. Always remember than an honorable secret committed is a thing sacred.

"I am about to commit to you two vital secrets of the Invisible Empire - the CS and PW. Do you swear to forever hold them in sacred secret reverence, even unto death?.....

"The CS and PW enables you to meet with and enjoy the fellowship of Klansmen in Klonklave assembled.

"For the present, and until changed, the CS is_____and the PW is_____.

"The Mioak, the sacred symbol of the Klan, is that (he explains what it is) by which Klansmen recognize each other without sword, sound or sign.

"I now present you with the material insignia of a Klansman, the sacred symbol of the Klan, by name the Mioak. Be faithful in its wearing. It must be worn on your person where it may be readily seen. Tell no person in the whole work what it is, its meaning and significance, even by hint or insinuation, as it is a positive secret of the Klan. Don't fail to recognize it by whomsoever it is worthily worn; always appreciate its sacred significance and be true to the same. As a test of your honor, I invest you with this symbol and commit to you its sacred secret."

He pins on the breast of the new Klansman the insignia and explains its symbolic meaning.

"You will now receive imperial instructions. Carefully preserve and seriously study this document and give earnest heed to same for on the practice of its teachings in your daily life depends your future advancement.

"You (or each of you), now are instructed Klansmen. Possessing all the rights, privileges and protection as such, will take your place with Klansmen in the sacred fellowship of the Invisible Empire."

The E.C. will then give two raps with his gavel, take his seat and proceed with the other business.

Lecture No. 1

-K-UNO-

The noble achievements of the American Knights of the Ku Klux Klan shine with undiminished effulgence through the gathering mist of accumulating years. An eloquent tribute to the chivalry and patriotism of the past, and the holy heroism of our fathers in preserving to us the sacred heritage of a superior race, - political supremacy, racial integrity, social peace and security, and to humanity the boon of cultured civilization, it abides the malicious slanders of the age, and is an inexhaustible source of inspiration to those of this generation who aspire to all things noble and good for themselves, our country and our race.

When the shuddering peals of the thunder of the impending storm of the American reconstruction were heard above the fading echoes of the battles of the great Civil War, the chosen victims stood aghast and pale, wondering at the meaning and purpose of the gathering gloom.

Darkness gathered apace and the demons were loosed from hell's most dismal depths; the blighting hand of devastation complete was laid heavy upon the Southern people - a people pauperized, bleeding, prostrated and defenseless. These noble people turned to the power of the national government for protection, but were spurned away with contempt and scorn. They had been promised protection in the possession of property, in the pursuit of peaceful employment and in every political and civil right formerly possessed by them as citizens of the national commonwealth. But the national government, by the shameful deviltry of its unscrupulous manipulators, repudiated that solemn promise and inaugurated the most disgraceful epoch in the annal of the nations against that unarmed, defeated, defenseless and submissive people.

This great people, defenseless and friendless, with a pestilence upon them more terrorizing than the seven plagues of Egypt, called to the nations of the earth. But none heard their cry. That call was a horrible medley full of intense anguish - melancholy groans of manly men struck dumb, mingling with the sickening, penetrating sobs of distressed woman and the plaintive cry of hungry, cladless child; on this melancholy orchestra grief touched the chords of universal sadness and displayed the direful dirge of death over the slaughtered corps of civilization.

Constitutional laws were stripped by profane hands of its virtuous vestments of civilized sovereignty of four thousand years in the making, and was mocked by polluted political pirates in legislative assemblies; and by the diabolical enactments of these assemblies, the hands on the dial of the clock of civilization in the tower of human progress were turned back thousands of years.

In the name of the law and national authority, the property of the husband and father was ruthlessly snatched from him without provocation by the venal hand of unholy confiscation; paupers by the multitude were made in a day. Carpetbaggers, the vultures of gluttonous greed, swooped down from their aerie on the lofty peaks of the mountains of national authority o'er the dismal plain of human helplessness, fasted their torturous talons in the fleece of defenseless innocence and consumed with avaricious avidity the vital flesh of the people's sustenance. And the scalawags - the conscienceless, cadaverous wolves of treason - gnawed the bones remaining to a baleful state of ghastly bleaching.

The chastity of the mother, wife, sister and daughter was imperiled and their sacred persons were placed in jeopardy to the licentious longings of lust-crazed beasts in form. Might ruled over right. Life and living was made intolerable; the rasping, discordant notes of penury had displaced the heavenly harmony of domestic happiness and no man's home was secure.

Ignorance, lust and hate seized the reins of state, and riot, raping and universal ruin reigned supreme. The highest form of cultured society was forced under the iron heel of pernicious passion who wielded a potent scepter of inquisitorial oppression, and the very blood of the Caucasian race was seriously threatened with an everlasting contamination.

QUESTIONS TO CANDIDATES

Each of the following questions must be answered by you (each of you) with an emphatic "Yes" or "No".

1st. Is the motive prompting your ambition to be a Klansman serious and unselfish?

2nd. Are you a native born or naturalized white, Christian American citizen?

3rd. Are you absolutely opposed to and free of any allegiance of any nature to any cause, government, people, sect or ruler that is foreign to the United States of America?

4th. Do you believe in the tenets of the Christian faith?

5th. Do you esteem the United States of America and its institutions above any other government, civil, political or ecclesiastical, in the whole world?

6th. Will you, without mental reservation, take a solemn oath to defend, preserve and enforce same?

7th. Do you believe in Klanishness and will you faithfully practice same towards Klansmen?

8th. Do you believe in and will you faithfully strive for the eternal maintenance of white supremacy?

9th. Will you faithfully obey our constitution and laws and conform willingly to

all usages, requirements and regulations?
    10th. Can you always be depended on?

You then administer Page 1, Section 1 and 2.

You will place your left hand over your heart and raise your right hand to heaven.
Oath of Allegiance
Section 1 Obedience
(You will say) "I" (pronounce your full name and repeat after me). "In the presence of God and man—most solemnly pledge, promise and swear—unconditionally—that I will faithfully obey—the constitution and laws—and will willingly conform to—all regulations, usages and requirements—of the American Knights of the Ku Klux Klan—which do now exist—or which may be hereafter enacted—and will render at all times—loyal respect and steadfast support—to the imperial authority of same—and will heartily heed—all official mandates—decrees—edicts—rulings and instructions—of the National Imperial Wizard thereof.—I will yield prompt response—to all summonses—I have knowledge of same—Providence alone preventing.
Section 2 Secrecy
"I most solemnly assert and affirm to keep sacredly secret—the signs, words and grip—and any and all other—matters and knowledge—of the K.K.K.—regarding which a most rigid secrecy—must be maintained—which may at any time—be communicated to me—and will never—divulge same nor even cause same to be divulged—to any person in the whole world—unless I know positively—that such person is a member of this order—in good and regular standing—and not even then—unless it be for the best interest of this Order.
"I most sacredly vow—and most positively swear—that I will never yield to bribe—flattery—threats—passion—punishment—persecution—persuasion—nor any enticements whatever—coming from or offered by—any person or persons—male or female—for the purpose of—obtaining from me—a secret or secret information—of the K.K.K.—I will die rather than divulge same—so help me God———Amen———"
You will drop your hands.
"Gentlemen (or Sirs): Ladies (or Madam): You will wait in patience and peace until you are informed of the decision of he E.C. and his or her Klansmen or Klanswomen in Klonklave assembled.

You will place your left hand over your heart and raise your right hand to heaven.
Oath of Allegiance
Sec. 3 Fidelity
(You will say) "I" (pronounce your full name and repeat after me). "Before God—and in the presence of—these mysterious Klansmen—on my sacred honor—do most solemnly and sincerely pledge—promise and swear—that I will diligently guard and faithfully foster—every interest of the American Knights of the Ku Klux Klan—and will maintain—its social cast and dignity.
"I swear that I will never recommend—any person for membership in this Order—whose mind is unsound—or whose reputation I know to be bad—or whose character is doubtful—or whose loyalty to our country—is in any way questionable.
"I swear that I will pay promptly—all just and legal demands—made upon me to defray the expenses—of my Unit and this Order—when same are due or called for.
"I swear that I will protect the property—of the American Knights of the Ku Klux Klan—of any nature whatsoever—and if any should be entrusted to my keeping—I will properly keep—or rightly use same—and will freely and promptly surrender same—or voluntarily discontinue—my membership in this Order.

"I swear that I will most determinedly—maintain peace and harmony—in all the deliberations—of the gatherings or assemblies—of the Invisible Empire—and of any subordinate jurisdiction—or Klan thereof.

"I swear that I will most strenuously—discourage selfishness—and selfish political ambition—on the part of myself or any Klansman.

"I swear that I will never allow—personal friendship—blood or family relationship—nor personal—political—or professional prejudice—malice nor ill will—to influence me in my vote—for the election or rejection—of an applicant—for membership in this Order—God being my helper——Amen——."

You will drop your hands.

You will place your left hand over your heart and raise your right hand to heaven.
Oath of Allegiance
Sec. 4 Klanishness
(You will say) "I" (pronounce your full name and repeat after me) "most solemnly pledge, promise and swear—that I will never slander—defraud—deceive—or in any manner wrong—the American Knights of the Ku Klux Klan—a Klansman—nor a Klansman's family—nor will I suffer the same to be done—if I can prevent it.

"I swear that I will be faithful—in defending and protecting—the home—reputation—and physical and business interest—of a Klansman's family.

"I swear that I will at any time—without hesitating—go to the assistance or rescue—of a Klansman in any way—at his call I will answer—I will be truly Klanish toward Klansmen—in all things honorable.

"I swear that I will never allow—any animosity—friction nor ill will—to arise and remain—between myself and a Klansman—but will be constant in my efforts—to promote real Klanishness—among the members of this Order.

"I swear that I will keep secure to myself—a secret of a Klansman—when same is committed to me—in the sacred bond of Klansman ship—the crime of violating this solemn oath—treason against the United States of America—rape—and malicious murder—alone excepted.

"I most solemnly assert and affirm—that to the government of the United States of America—and any state thereof—of which I may become a resident—I sacredly swear—an unqualified allegiance—above any other and every kind of government—in the whole world—I here and now pledge my life—my property—my vote—and my sacred honor—to uphold its flag—its constitution—and constitutional laws—and will protect—defend—and enforce same unto death.

"I most solemnly promise and swear—that I will always, at all times and in all place—help, aid and assist—the duly constituted officers of the law—in the proper performance of their legal duties.

"I swear that I will most zealously—an valiantly—shield and preserve—by any and all—justifiable means and methods—the sacred constitutional rights—and privileges of—free public schools—free speech—separation of church and state—liberty—white supremacy—just laws—and the pursuit of happiness—against any encroachment—of any nature—by any person or persons—political party or parties—religious sect or people—native, naturalized or foreign—of any race—color—creed—lineage or tongue whatsoever.

"All to which I have sworn by this oath—I will seal with my blood—be Thou my witness—Almighty God——Amen——"

You will drop your hands.

Next you will knight your new members and give a welcoming speech.

Officer Robe Color & Stripes

1. National and/or Imperial Offices (5) stripes on the sleeves
2. State and/or Grand Offices (4) stripes on the sleeves.
3. County and State assistants (3) stripes on the sleeves.
4. County assistants (2) stripes on the sleeves
5. County Secretary (1) stripe on the sleeve - no authority other than office.

Office	Robe	Stripes/Sleeves	Cape
Nat. Imperial Wizard	Purple	Gold	Gold-Under
Imperial Kladd	Gold	White, Orange, Green, Purple, Red/on sleeves and on bottom of robe	Cape-Gold
Imperial Klabee		None-Robe-Secretive	
Klokan	White	Purple	Purple-Under
Imperial E.C.	Black	Orange	Orange-Under
Grand Dragon	White	Green	Green-Under
State-Hydra	White	Green	White
E.C.	White	Orange	Orange-Under
Klaliff	White	Orange	White
Kilgrapp	White	Orange	White
Great Titan	Black	(4) Green	Green-Under

Bottom stripes are earned!!! First of all you receive one when you become an officer. Second, the Imperial Office, unless stated otherwise, allows one stripe for every five years of service to the Order. All members who have joined the American Knights from other Klans, their service years are transferable. If you have the wrong number of stripes on your sleeves or on the bottom, you need to correct the error.

Selected Bibliography

Chalmers, David M. *Hooded Americanism: The History of the Ku Klux Klan*, 1981, Franklin Watts

Coppola, Vincent *Dragons of God: A Journey Through Far-Right America*, 1997, Longstreet Press

Davidson, Osha G. *The Best of Enemies: From Prejudice to Friendship in the Post Civil-Rights South*, 1996, Simon & Schuster

Davis, Daryl *Klan-Destine Relationships: A Black Man's Odyssey in the Ku Klux Klan*, 1997, New Horizon Press Publishers

Dobratz, Betty A. and Shanks-Meile, Stephanie L. *"White Power, White Pride!" The White Separatist Movement in the United Staves*, 1997, Twayne Publishers, Simon and Schuster Macmillan

Lutholtz, M. William *Grand Dragon: D. C. Stephenson and the Ku Klux Klan in Indiana*, 1991, Purdue University Press

Moore, Leonard J. *Citizen Klansmen: The Ku Klux Klan in Indiana, 1921-1928*, 1991, The University of North Carolina Press

Ruiz, Jim *The Black Hood of the Ku Klux Klan*, 1997, Austin & Winfield

Sims, Patsy *The Klan*, 1997, University Press of Kentucky

The Author

Worth H. Weller is a journalist and photographer.

A 1968 graduate of Duke University, he was scooped up by Uncle Sam the following year. After completing the US Army Signal Corps Photography School he spent most of his three-year hitch in Europe, photographing people from Helsinki to Istanbul.

In 1974 he began his career as a Hoosier newspaper editor, editing a prize-winning weekly newspaper since then. In 1996 his photo series on the modern Ku Klux Klan received the top journalism prize in Indiana.

Photographs that Weller took in Nicaragua during the Contra war have won exhibition prizes, as have his photos from the aftermath of the civil war in El Salvador and from his three trips to Chiapas, Mexico.

Weller is also an award winning writer, with a host of articles over the years receiving honors from the Hoosier State Press Association and the Indiana Society for Professional Journalists. He presently is completing a book about the conflict in Chiapas.

The author in Guatemala, 1996

Index